Making sense of

Generation Y

The world view of 15- to 25-year-olds

Making sense of
Generation Y
The world view of 15- to 25-year-olds

Sara Savage, Sylvia Collins-Mayo, Bob Mayo
with Graham Cray

CHURCH HOUSE
PUBLISHING

Church House Publishing
Church House
Great Smith Street
London SW1P 3NZ

Tel: 020 7898 1451
Fax: 020 7898 1449

ISBN-13 978 0 7151 4051 2
ISBN-10 0 7151 4051 5

Published 2006 by Church House Publishing

The opinions expressed in this book are those of the authors and do not
necessarily reflect the official policy of the General Synod or
The Archbishops' Council of the Church of England.

Cover design by Andy Stonehouse

Typeset in Rotis Semi Sans by RefineCatch Limited, Bungay, Suffolk

Printed by Creative Print and Design Group, Ebbw Vale

Contents

Contents

About the authors

Sylvia Collins-Mayo teaches at Kingston University. She completed her PhD on young people's faith at the University of Surrey in 1997. Her post-doctoral research has continued to focus on the relationship between young people and religion. She is currently researching the role of Christian-based youth work on the spiritual development of unchurched young people.

Graham Cray is Bishop of Maidstone, Chairman of the Soul Survivor Trust, and one of the founders of the Centre for Youth Ministry. He was Chairman of the 'Mission-shaped Church' working party. As Principal of Ridley Hall, he commissioned the research which forms the basis of this book.

Bob Mayo was, for a number of years, the Director of the Cambridge Centre for Youth Ministry at Ridley Hall. He is now the Vicar of St Stephen and St Thomas Church, a parish in Shepherds Bush, in inner city London. He combines practical face-to-face work with young people with research through the Nazareth Project into how youth and community work might raise a Christian awareness among Generation Y. He is the author of *Gospel Exploded* (1996) and *Ambiguous Evangelism* (2004).

Sara Savage is Senior Research Associate with the Psychology and Christianity Project, Faculty of Divinity, University of Cambridge (www.divinity.cam.ac.uk/pcp/), and lecturer in the Cambridge Theological Federation. Sara is co-author of *Psychology for Christian Ministry* (Watts, Nye & Savage, 2002). Her other publications include articles and chapters on fundamentalism, church consultancy, pastoral care, the future of the parish system, and the arts. Sara is the developer of the Beta course, a multimedia, video-based pastoral care course for developing churches as caring communities (www.beta-course.org). A dancer and choreographer for many years, Sara is a practitioner of the arts in ministry, and is married to an Anglican vicar.

Foreword

The Church's mission to young people is close to my heart. In my previous diocese, Birmingham, I set up a vibrant Bishop's Youth Council to plan youth events. Their work on youth evangelism through the B-Cent, B-Sent and B-Scent Programme was breathtaking.[1]

It is self-evident to me that in order to engage with young people, we must hear what they are saying. What matters to them? How do they shape their world? What does their spirituality look like?

This important book does us a great service in giving us an insight into the world view of 'Generation Y'. What it reveals is the 'large mismatch' between the world view of those aged 15–25 and the Church. The research described in this book suggests that young people are happy with life as it is, that they have no felt need for a 'transcendent something else', and that they regard the Church as boring and irrelevant.

Thankfully, however, this book also provides some pointers as to how the Church might begin to address this situation. This book notes that 'the Christian faith often has little relevance simply because it is largely unknown'. It stresses the need for investment in relationships with young people and for 'patient sowing' of the gospel story into our culture. There are no 'instant solutions', but there are things we, empowered by the Holy Spirit, can – and must – do.

The task is urgent. I commend this book as a starting point for those wanting to proclaim Christ afresh in this generation.

+ Sentamu Ebor

---

[1] More information can be found on: www.b-cent.com

Preface

For Generation Y, born after 1980, Margaret Thatcher is a piece of social history, relationships happen over the Internet and music marks their territory. How does this generation think about the world? What does their spirituality look like?

Given this generation's unprecedented immersion in popular culture, we examined how young people make sense of the world and themselves through the popular arts. The disparity between the world views of young people and the Church is such that few doubt the urgent need for the Church to revive genuine communication with young people. This book represents our effort to help bridge this gap, based on a two-year research project.

Our aims were to discover:

- the ways in which the popular arts are consumed, understood and interpreted by young people in their day-to-day living;
- how the popular arts are being used by young people to shape a world view;
- the nature of young people's spirituality.

We spoke to 124 young people around England in youth clubs, colleges and universities. While we cannot claim our sample was representative of all young people, the sample did reflect some of the main demographic characteristics of English youth:

- 52% were female; 48% were male.
- 94% were White; 6% were Black or Asian.
- 60% defined themselves as non-Christian; 40% as Christian.

Our aim was to elucidate the world view of these young people by drawing out their relationship to the popular arts (soaps, film, music and clubbing, advertising and culturally iconic images). We asked for their views on the latest storyline in *EastEnders*, what they felt when they went clubbing on a Friday evening, what they thought of the latest Benetton adverts.

The results were not what we, or the Church, expected!

The shape of this book

Readers may want different things from this book. If you are in a hurry and want to come straight to the point – how young people make sense of the world via the popular arts – read Chapter 3. General principles for youth work based on our research are found in Chapter 7. We hope many readers will stay with us for the whole journey.

Part One

Chapters 1 and 2 give an overview of research carried out on youth, religion, spirituality, and popular culture. At the end of Chapter 2, we set out our research method in more detail. Chapter 3 provides a summary of our findings.

Part Two

Chapters 4, 5 and 6 immerse the reader in young people's world view, and how this is sustained by the creative way young people use the popular arts. Chapter 4 explores the worlds of soaps and film, and the role story plays in how young people make sense of the world. Chapter 5 looks at how music spills into every area of young people's lives. Chapter 6 unpacks the potential of symbol and image to engage young people's spirituality.

Part Three

We discuss the implications of the research for youth work and youth ministry in Chapter 7, and Bishop Graham Cray unfolds the implications for the wider Church in Chapters 8 and 9.

Throughout the study we have tried to reproduce our interviewees' own words so that their 'voice' may be heard. Names, however, have been changed to protect the identities of the young people.

Acknowledgements

Our sincere thanks to all the young people involved in this project. They were the catalyst for the sheer fun of working together, interweaving our different disciplines: psychology, sociology, theology and youth work. The research emerged from and generated deep and real friendships.

Special thanks are due to Revd Professor Jeremy Begbie, Director of Theology through the Arts, for his oversight of the whole project, and his diplomatic and precise guidance. None of this would have been possible without the Mercers' Company, who were kind enough to provide the funding to make this project a reality, and who have expressed a close and intense interest in the project from the beginning. Special thanks are due to the Master, Wing Commander Mike Dudgeon, and to David Vermont, Charles Parker and Pia Crowley.

We are also grateful to our editor Tracey Messenger, and to Liz Gulliford, Christine for her transcriptions, Jane Chevous, Jane Hildreth, Revd Dr Fraser Watts, Revd Mark Savage and Andy Lloyd for their help and support throughout the research and writing. We would also like to thank all those who read and commented on draft versions of the text, including Craig Abbott, Paul Bayes, Lynda Barley, Andy Poole and Mike Powis.

PART ONE:
THE WORLD VIEW OF GENERATION Y

1

Young people and the Church

Take a walk down any high street and you will find the supernatural on sale. You can buy glow-in-the-dark crosses, Kabbalah bracelets, Harry Potter books. Read a newspaper for your daily horoscope; turn on the television for celebrity endorsements of yoga: popular culture is oozing with spirituality. Yet enter a church on an average Sunday and chances are it will be at least half empty. This is particularly so if the church lacks young people in their teens or early twenties.

Young people are a litmus test for a church's viability. In 1998, only 7 per cent of 15- to 19-year-olds, and 5 per cent of 20- to 29-year-olds went to church on a Sunday.[1] Meanwhile, church decline continues. Does the spiritual sensibility of young people now lie outside the Church and inside the cinemas and nightclubs of popular culture?

Our task was to discover to what extent young people make sense of themselves and their world through the popular arts – that milieu in which youth live, move and have their being. We wondered what young people's world view and spirituality look like. We wondered whether – a wild hope! – the popular arts could resource the Church to 'do' theology in meaningful ways.

To try to answer these questions we began a research project into the world view of Generation Y, those aged 15 to 25. Three researchers, a Christian psychologist (Sara Savage), a sociologist of religion (Sylvia Collins-Mayo) and a theologian and expert in youth and community work (Bob Mayo), together analysed young people's conversations as they responded to music, clubbing, films, TV soaps and culturally iconic images.

The next chapters describe the socially shared world in which these young people are immersed, unveiling a large mismatch between the Church's and young people's world view. Our aim, from the outset, was to help the Church listen to young people in order to regain an authentic relationship with them.

This book presents the findings and conclusions of our study. In Part One we set out the broad picture of young people's world view, the general significance of popular art and culture to them, and their religious and spiritual sensibility. We present our research method and an overview of our findings. In Part Two we look more closely at young people's world view arising from their interaction with specific aspects of popular culture. In Part Three we discuss principles for youth work that emerge as a result of our research and Bishop Graham Cray reflects on the implications that the world view of Generation Y has for the Church.

We begin by setting out the background to our study and defining the terms we will be using.

Young people and generations

Let us clarify what we mean by 'young people' and 'Generation Y'. The terms 'youth' and 'young people' conjure up many images. Young people are seen as creative, beautiful, enthusiastic, carefree, passionate, energetic, fun, full of potential and hope for the future. The Anglican Church's report, *Youth A Part* reminds us of the way young people's accomplishments contribute to society.[2] At the same time, young people are also seen as moody, rebellious, vulnerable, troubled, troublesome and dangerous. Newspaper headlines draw attention to the high rate of teenage pregnancies, young male suicides, teenage drug and alcohol problems, youth homelessness, and violence committed by and upon young people. All of these views are true of some young people, some of the time. The diversity of images indicates how difficult it is to pin down 'young people' as a single group.

Age as a marker of youth is itself subject to increasing flexibility. In our study we were primarily interested in young people in their late teens and early twenties. But if youth is regarded as a period of transition between dependent childhood and independent adulthood then, due to changes in social structures and attitudes, a person can be described as 'young' right up to their thirties. Traditional markers of adulthood such as entering the labour market, establishing a settled partnership or marriage, having children and setting up a home, are generally occurring later in life than they were 20 or 30 years ago. At the lower end of the age range, the 'tweenage' group (10- to 13-year-olds) seems to have much in common with older teens in terms of consumer interest and spending power. Young people can therefore be anything from 11 to 30 years old.

Given such social diversity, how can we talk about young people as a coherent social group? It is here that we find the idea of generations particularly helpful. Generations can be understood in a number of ways,[3] but here we draw on Karl Mannheim's[4] view that a 'generation' refers to a group of people who experience and respond to specific socio-historical conditions in common ways, depending in part on age. In other words, people growing up, living through and responding to particular historical events, political structures, dominant ideologies and technical developments together form a generation with a shared world view that distinguishes them from other generations. For Mannheim, it is the events, ideas and experiences encountered by young people between the ages of 17 to 25 that particularly shape their generation. Writers differ in terms of the labels and birth year boundaries they apply to particular generations, but they are usually periods of about 20 years. For the twentieth century, Hilborn and Bird use the names and characteristics below.[5]

- **The World War Generation** (also known as the GI Generation in the United States – born 1901–24). This generation's self-understanding and view of the world was shaped by their experience of two world wars separated by a period of economic depression and reconstruction. It has been argued that the World War Generation was characterized by confidence, having witnessed advances in science, medicine and technology, but it was also essentially a conformist generation where young people joined movements such as the Boy Scouts and Girl Guides and traditional patterns of social order were preferred. Prominent ideologies for the World War Generation were 'modernism, scientific progressivism, Marxism, socialism, Freudianism, existentialism and capitalism'.[6]
- **Builder Generation** (also known as the Silent Generation – born 1925–45). Builders had much in common with their parents and in many ways consolidated their parents' achievements and continued building the future after World War II. It has been suggested that Builders tended towards conservative tastes, but at the same time they were also the first generation to have a recognizable 'teen age', marked by the development of a youth market in the 1950s based on music, fashion and entertainment – a market that has grown into the popular arts and culture we are interested in today, and a market which has helped define 'youth' as a concept ever since. Post-war affluence was key to this development of youth consumerism. It enabled the rapid expansion of the popular music industry, the invention of 'teenpics' in cinemas and the development of

youth-orientated television. Like the generation before, the prominent ideologies for the Builder Generation were 'modernism, scientific progressivism, Marxism, socialism, Freudianism, existentialism and capitalism'.[7]

- **Boomer Generation** (so called because the birth rate increased after World War II creating a 'baby boom' – born 1946–63). Boomers are usually characterized by the counter-culture of the 1960s. Disillusioned with traditional institutions and authorities (including the Church), young Boomers began to look for new, authentic ways of living. Their focus was on the immediacy of experiences, and the values of freedom, self-realization and autonomy. They were a liberal, idealistic and optimistic generation; politically active, looking forward to a future of peace, love and prosperity without the constraints society imposed on their parents. They were the first young people to have access to the contraceptive pill, and (the middle class at least) to benefit from the expansion of higher education. Later they would also make use of the relaxation of the divorce laws in the 1960s. It has been observed that the Boomers were the first to be generationally conscious and aware of a gap between their values and ways of living compared to that of their parents. This generation gap was primarily expressed through popular music. Prominent ideologies for the Boomer Generation included 'modernism, scientific progressivism, Marxism, socialism, secularism, free-market capitalism, free expression, individualism, and "DIY" spirituality'.[8]

- **Generation X** (sometimes called the Buster Generation because there was a small dip in the birth rate after the Boomers – born 1964–81). Generation X picked up the legacy of the Boomers and in some ways paid the price of their experimentation with the counter-culture. Generation X were the latchkey kids who saw the divorce rate rise among their parents and the AIDS epidemic spread among their peers. Generation X also grew up through an economic recession where unemployment was a reality faced by many young people. Consequently, Generation X lost much of the optimistic idealism of the Boomers and instead developed a more pragmatic approach to life. Popular art and culture has been a central factor in Generation X's life, and advances in information and communications technology has contributed to the postmodern outlook that we are increasingly familiar with today. Prominent ideologies of Generation X include 'postmodernism, free-market capitalism, consumerism, pluralism, tolerance, individualism, spiritual eclecticism and introversion, New Age, eco-awareness, communitarianism, globalism'.[9]

This takes us to Generation Y, today's young people and the subject of this book:

- **Generation Y** (also known as the Millennial Generation – born 1982 onwards). Generation Y has grown up in a globalized society where many of the limitations of time and space have been overcome by further advances in information and communications technology. In this respect Generation Y is a technological generation that takes computers, emailing, text messaging and the Internet for granted. This is particularly interesting from our point of view since the digital revolution has enabled the further expansion and diversification of popular culture. A young person living in Britain today can access hip hop in South Africa and a young person in India enjoy the latest American soap operas. Cultures from across the world are fragmented, appropriated and reinterpreted in other contexts to form new hybrid cultures – a process some theorists have called 'glocalization', meaning the 'global production of the local and the localization of the global'.[10] Under these circumstances there is a growing potential for cultural homogenization at a global level but also, conversely, the defence and re-entrenchment of traditional cultural identities at the local level. The events of 11 September 2001 emphasize the potential of the latter.

As well as creating new cultural resources, globalization and technology have altered the labour market for Generation Y young people in Britain. Manual, unskilled work which supported many working-class young people in previous generations has declined or been outsourced to other parts of the world. Young people are therefore encouraged to stay on in further and higher education to equip themselves for an economy that requires a skilled and flexible labour force. Consequently the numbers of young people who continue with post-compulsory education in Britain has increased over the last ten years, while those who choose to leave school at 16 often end up unemployed or in unstable jobs within the service industries.

But young people's outlook on life does not appear to be bleak. Studies indicate that many young people accept the uncertainties of employment.[11] Indeed, they positively embrace them and say they would find a job for life boring. In this respect Generation Y appears to be quite a self-reliant, confident and upbeat generation. They also seem to be tolerant and community minded, a generation of young people who value their family and friends, and on the whole intend to marry and have a family of their own. Indeed, Generation Y appears to be quite traditional and conservative in a number of core areas of life,[12] as we shall see later on in our own exploration of Generation Y's world view.

We hope it is clear from the above, that the idea of generations is a helpful way of mapping young people in society. However, as already mentioned, young people are not all the same, and within generations we can expect young people to understand and experience their society differently according to background and demographic characteristics such as gender, class, ethnicity, sexual orientation, and so on. With this in mind we found it appropriate to think in terms of generational *units*[13] – subgroups within the wider generation. Thus, while a 16-year-old White working-class boy and an 18-year-old middle-class Asian girl might share some ideas in common by virtue of the fact that they have been subject to the same socio-historical period, and may even have lived as part of the same school community or neighbourhood, their outlook on life is likely to be different because they come from different subgroups within the generation.

In our study of Generation Y, our focus was on a particular unit within that generation: 'socially included', mainly White, young men and women. These young people have enough money to consume and participate in popular arts and culture; they have some connection with mainstream institutions such as youth clubs, colleges and universities. We believe these 'included' young people provide a good barometer of wider society, although youth research has sometimes neglected them in favour of the more marginal, excluded and problematic young people.

Popular culture and world views

Popular arts, popular culture and world views are flexible concepts which need some pinning down. Just how widespread an art form has to be in order to be regarded as popular is a moot point, but the relationship with the mass media is a close one. Popular culture can be contrasted with high culture,[14] which is usually accessed by (and often only accessible to) a wealthy minority that on the whole excludes young people.[15] For our purposes, popular culture includes all those art forms (such as music, dance, visual imagery, storytelling, design, etc.) that are shared by large numbers of people in everyday life. They include Hollywood films, soap operas, popular music, clubbing, advertising, fashion, magazines and popular fiction.

Like the popular arts, world views are collective entities. By 'world view' we mean the shared framework of beliefs, knowledge and understanding through which young people experience the world. They use this 'lens' to make sense of their lives. Every human being has a world view that is, in part, inherited from wider society and in part shaped according to individual and local circumstance. World views both enable and constrain us in our life choices and social actions. They provide the common knowledge that generates our expectations for the future, but also sets limits to our horizons. Because world view knowledge and understanding is generally implicit, world views tend to go largely unexamined on a day-to-day basis. This makes them difficult to research.

A world view is generally only made visible when it is challenged. In this respect, cultural theorists talk about world views as operating at different levels. A 'dominant world view' embraces the majority of society while often reflecting the particular interests of the ruling elite. This can be challenged or subverted by secondary world views held by smaller groups who make sense of their lives according to different norms and assumptions. In contemporary society we are used to the idea of a plurality of world views jostling for attention.

At a deep level, whether we are directly conscious of it or not, world views embrace perceptions of reality and identity. They address ultimate questions in life (e.g., 'Who are we?' 'What is the purpose of life?' 'Does God exist?') and provide explanations as to why things are the way they are. World views embody values, shape priorities and define what really matters. They inform notions of morality and the principles of relationship. In other words, at their core, world views deal with the questions and concerns that have traditionally been seen as the province of religion. To put it another way, Walsh and Middleton suggest at the heart of any world view is a 'faith commitment':

> What is a faith commitment? It is the way we answer four basic questions facing everyone: (1) *Who am I?* Or, what is the nature, task and purpose of human beings? (2) *Where am I?* Or, what is the nature of the world and universe I live in? (3) *What's wrong?* Or, what is the basic problem or obstacle that keeps me from attaining fulfilment? In other words, how do I understand evil? And (4) *What is the remedy?* Or, how is it possible to overcome this hindrance to my fulfilment? In other words, how do I find salvation?[16]

Tom Wright, whose work we found particularly helpful in structuring our research design (see Chapter 2), makes much the same point:

> worldviews provide the *stories* through which human beings view reality ... from these stories one can in principle discover how to answer the basic *questions* that determine human

existence: who are we, where are we, what is wrong, and what is the solution?[17]

All cultures cherish deep-rooted beliefs which can in principle be called up to answer these questions. All cultures (that is) have a sense of identity, of environment, of a problem with the way the world is, and of a way forward – a redemptive eschatology, to be more precise – which will, or may, lead out of that problem.[18]

Answers to these existential questions at the heart of a world view give people a socially shared reality in which they can put their trust, a basis upon which their actions make sense and hope for tomorrow is maintained. Of course, until relatively recently these questions were answered at a societal level in Britain by the Church. Now much of the Church's influence has been lost. What, then, has taken its place as the source of ultimate meaning, particularly for young people? To what extent has popular culture taken over as a main resource of meaning for British youth? Does it match what Tom Beaudoin suggests for Generation X in the United States?

During our lifetimes, especially during the critical period of the 1980s, pop culture was the amniotic fluid that sustained us. For a generation of kids who had a fragmented or completely broken relationship to 'formal' or 'institutional' religion, pop culture filled the spiritual gaps.[19]

This takes us to our third point for clarification: the difference between religion and spirituality.

Religion and spirituality

Of all our attempts to clarify terms, pinning down 'religion' and 'spirituality' has been the hardest. We are not alone in this difficulty. Rose, for example, was prompted to ask the question: 'Is the term "spirituality" a word that everybody uses but nobody knows what anyone means by it?'[20] One thing that does appear to be clear, however, is that spirituality has a better press than religion:

Religion tends to be associated with what is publicly available, such as churches, mosques, Bibles, prayer books, religious officials, weddings and funerals. It also regularly includes uncomfortable associations with boredom, narrow-mindedness and being out of date, as well as more disconcerting links with fanaticism, bigotry, cruelty, and persecution. It seems that in many people's minds religion is firmly caught up in the cold brutalities of history.

Spirituality is almost always seen as much warmer, associated with love, inspiration, wholeness, depth, mystery and personal devotions like prayer and meditation.[21]

According to Hay's findings, 'religion' is very much linked in the popular mind with public institutions and social practices, and 'spirituality' with private practices and the subjective world 'within' – which may or may not be connected with institutional religion.[22] In this respect spirituality tends to subsume religion. The social sciences also make the same basic distinction between public religion and private spirituality, albeit without the value judgements held by the people in Hay's study. Beyond this basic distinction, however, there are some extra points to bear in mind.

In terms of 'religion', there are two schools of thought within the social sciences. For some theorists, adopting a 'substantive' approach to the study of religion, religious beliefs, practices and experiences, by definition, have to have an explicit connection with a transcendent or supernatural reality. Thus Christianity is 'religious' because it contains an explicit belief in God, it has a set of rituals which help connect the believer with that transcendent reality, and it provides moral guidance for living life in the light of that belief. Other theorists, however, broaden the definition of religion to include all those beliefs and practices that perform a religious *function*, usually the function of binding people together into a community and enabling them to make sense of their lives. According to this view, even apparently secular social phenomena can be described as 'invisible' religion[23] or 'implicitly' religious[24] if they fulfil the required functions.

Walsh and Middleton's idea that world views have an essentially religious core because they address basic existential questions is an example of a functional approach to religion. Similarly some political ideologies might be described as 'religious' in their function, or, as we shall see in Chapter 2, some forms of popular culture. The beauty of functional definitions is that they allow us to identify new forms of religiosity that may be developing in contemporary society, which may otherwise go unnoticed. The downside is that since almost anything can serve a religious function the term risks losing analytical worth.

Equally, we need to be careful when talking about spirituality. If anything, 'spirituality' is an even more slippery term than 'religion'. The National Youth Agency's consultation paper on this topic describes spirituality as an 'essential part of our true humanity' yet acknowledges it 'has been virtually impossible to come up with an absolute, clean definition of spirituality which can be used in every circumstance'.[25] Some theorists equate spirituality with religion, others suggest religion and spirituality are similar but not identical and that it is possible to be spiritual without being religious (and vice versa). Sheldrake places spirituality 'on the frontier between religious experience and inherited tradition'.[26]

Formative and transformative spirituality

Faced with all this ambiguity we find it helpful when thinking about spirituality to use a two-pronged approach, similar to our discussion of religion. The first approach to spirituality, like implicit religion, is a broad definition that sees spirituality as a fundamental potential within the human condition, thus inherent in a world view. In this sense spirituality focuses on an individual's sense of raised awareness of relationality (with, for example, self and others, and possibly God, the universe, etc.), which may include mystery sensing (awe, wonder, dread), meaning making and value sensing (delight and despair, right and wrong, existential meaning).[27] We call this 'formative' spirituality because it is inherent in the human condition. Spirituality in this sense is implicit in many individual actions and experiences (appreciation of the natural world or a painting, loving and delighting in family and friends, feeling passionate about a social or environmental cause, expressing one's identity, etc.). However, these phenomena may not be recognized by the individual as spiritual, or the spiritual aspect of them may be of little consequence to the individual concerned.

A narrower concept of spirituality is more akin to theological discussions on the subject and the substantive approaches to religion mentioned above. This narrower definition of spirituality, which we call 'transformative', involves a conscious attempt to develop beyond formative spirituality in order to touch a deeper reality or a transcendent realm. Transformative spirituality involves the individual in deliberate practices (whether overtly 'religious' or not) which aim to foster mindfulness of the Other (howsoever conceived – e.g., God, Self, Universe) and help maintain a sense of connectedness. This spiritual mindfulness then has significance for the individual in so far as it permeates daily life, guides his or her decisions and provides a continued appreciation of the Other. When people describe themselves as 'spiritual seekers', we understand this to be engaging with transformative spirituality. Rose's analysis of how the term 'spirituality' is used by people whose professional work engages with a spiritual dimension (authors, teachers, psychologists and religious leaders) fits well with our idea of transformative spirituality:

> What seems to be prerequisite [for 'spirituality'] are three criteria: firstly, even though many respondents pointed out that particular kinds of spirituality do not have to be religious, some form of continued reverential experience, that is, experience of (or relating to) the numinous or matters of ultimate concern; secondly, some type of maintained effort regarding practice, for example, living in accord with a particular convention, such as the Ten Commandments, the Noble Eightfold Path, or other less formalized codes, such as the Pagan ethic; lastly, a life imbued with love, that is, filled with altruistic activities and loving-kindness.[28]

Transformative spirituality may, potentially, be realized in a number of ways. For example, through participation in traditional religions or through practices which Heelas and Woodhead et al. place under the heading of the 'holistic milieu': 'yoga, reiki, meditation, tai chi, aromatherapy, much paganism, rebirthing, reflexology, much wicca and many more'.[29]

Our research agenda was to see how, if at all, popular culture contributed to either of these spiritual dimensions of young people's world view and, in particular, whether or not it enabled them to engage in any form of transformative spirituality.

If the Church is no longer seen by many young people today as a source of transformative spirituality, what is? We turn now to research on young people's attitudes to the Church.

Young people's relationships with the Church

There are plenty of figures to show the Church has limited appeal to young people today. In terms of church attendance between 1979 and 1998 the number of children and young people up to 19 years of age in church on an average Sunday fell by around 50 per cent, and the number of 20- to 29-year-olds dropped by 45 per cent.[30] Similarly, Sunday school attendance has declined. Jackson points out that for 'every 100 children who were in

Sunday school in 1930 ... there are only 9 today'.[31] The number of baptisms and confirmations is also falling.

The decline in church attendance among young people is a continuation of a trend set by previous generations (which actually encompasses all types of institutional affiliation, not just religious institutions). There has been a progressive atrophying of the churchgoing habit, particularly since the 1960s. This means that today there is neither the expectation that young people will go to church, nor a pattern of churchgoing for young people to follow. Even if young people want to go to church, the generational decline in church attendance means that there is a shortage of adults with the necessary knowledge and skills to accommodate them.[32] It is not surprising then that Francis's survey of 33,000 13- to 15-year-olds in England and Wales during the 1990s, showed that 51 per cent of young people felt they could be a Christian without going to church (see Table 1.1).

Moreover, young people's attitudes and expectations of church do not encourage them to attend. There is an expectation that church will be boring and devoid of personal meaning.[33] Its moral teachings (particularly those concerned with sexuality) are often perceived to be at odds with the young people's own sense of right and wrong.[34] Young people hate the hypocrisy they see in some churchgoers who do not practise the love that they preach. On the rare occasions that young people do go to church they often feel no connection with other members of the congregation who are usually a lot older than them, and whose expression of faith does not match the young people's stage of development – church services sometimes demand too much of young people.[35]

All of these attitudes militate against churchgoing among the young. So too does the array of competing activities available on Sundays. An even greater barrier may be the bullying and ridicule that young churchgoers sometimes face from their non-churchgoing peers.[37] The point that churchgoing is not

Table 1.1 Young people's views on church from Francis's study[36]

	Yes (%)	? (%)	No (%)
I believe that I can be a Christian without going to church	51	32	18
The Church seems irrelevant to life today	28	44	28
I want my children to be baptized/christened in church	54	27	19
I want to get married in church	73	19	8
Church is boring	52	26	22
Church ministers/vicars/priests do a good job	36	46	18

'cool' was amply made by a group of 17- and 18-year-olds we spoke to shortly after completing our research, most of whom had some past experience of church. When asked to describe church they responded:

> 'Cardigans'; 'Sandals and socks'; 'Old, peaceful, decorative'; 'Corrupt, having somewhat lost the plot'; 'Marginally pointless, traditionalist, past its sell-by date'; 'Unchanging, stagnant, charitable'; 'Church is no longer seen by the majority of youth as a place of hope, just as an institution that is not the answer'; 'Car boot sales are better.'

However, it is not all bad news as far as young people and the Church are concerned. For one thing, their limited church experience means that young people may be freer to experience what the Church has to offer should they ever venture through its doors. The young people in Francis's study also remained loyal to the Church as a vehicle by which to celebrate rites of passage. Seventy-three per cent said they would want to get married in church, and while this could easily be put down to tradition and wanting the wedding to look 'right' it is harder to dismiss the 54 per cent of young people wanting their children to be baptized or christened. Our discussions with young people also indicate that some believe church can have a positive impact on attenders, albeit that it was not for them personally:

> 'Church gives people peace'; 'It provides a place to show their devotion in public'; 'It gives a sense of unity with other believers, a sense of community and mutual support'; 'It helps people to live better lives'; 'It is often meaningful to those who do go'; 'It's for people who need a physical representation of hope in order to put meaning into their lives.'

> Church is for: 'People who want to feel holy'; 'People who want to belong'; 'People who are looking for answers, including answers to moral dilemmas, and for direction in life.'

Moreover, while they are in a minority, there are some very committed young churchgoers. In Francis's, study around 14 per cent of young people attended church on a weekly basis.[38] These churchgoers were more likely to feel they had a purpose in life than the other young people, and only 24 per cent felt church was boring.[39] In this respect we might argue that churches *do* meet some of the spiritual and social needs of some young people. Furthermore, Jackson draws attention to the apparent success of faith-based youth and children's work (Crusaders and Kidz Klub) when the meeting time was changed from a Sunday to a Thursday evening and therefore not competing with other activities.[40] Moreover, among churches that employ professional youth workers, the exodus of young people from the church is slower than for churches without these key workers.

On an individual level, committed young Christians confirm the importance of the faith community in churches and parachurch organizations as a means to help them sustain their faith. Hervieu-Léger found young Catholics in France attached a lot of importance to hearing testimonies, recognizing a shared culture and talking about their faith with peers while on pilgrimage to a World Youth Gathering in Poland in 1991.[41]

Finally, it is worth registering the rise of neo-orthodox Christian groups to which some young people seem to be attracted in the United States.[42] The all-embracing purposeful lifestyle offered by these churches appeals to young people who want an authentic, meaningful faith. Although the church culture in the United States is rather different from that in Britain, conservative churches, particularly those that embrace charismatic spirituality, which engage the emotions as well as the rational mind, seem to have more appeal to young people than those of a more liberal and non-charismatic persuasion.

In sum, while the Church does not have any meaningful contact with the majority of young people, it still has the capacity to help those it does engage with towards transformative spirituality, particularly through some of its dedicated youth programmes.

The Church's relationship with young people

The Church is, of course, well aware that it has little significant contact with most young people, and that a gap exists between youth and church cultures. There has also been a recognition of the increasing age profile of church ministers – at the time of writing, half of all Anglican incumbents are over 51.[43] In response to this situation there has been a rapid expansion of the number of youth workers employed through churches, paralleled by the development of specialized youth and community work training through organizations such as the Centre for Youth Ministry, Oasis and Moorlands.

The Church's work with young people now happens through the parallel but overlapping disciplines of 'youth ministry' and 'youth and community work'. Youth ministry is an explicitly faith-based activity. It works from the assumption of a shared knowledge base about the Christian faith and sees its role as being to disciple, guide and even socialize young people into the faith. Youth and community work, on the other hand, essentially consists of informal educational activities designed to help young people reflect on their experiences and use them to develop and grow as individuals. In our terms, youth ministry tends to focus on transformative spirituality, whereas youth and community work is primarily working with formative spirituality.

Ward[44] described the difference between youth ministry and youth and community work as being 'inside-out' versus 'outside-in' youth work. 'Inside-out' youth ministry works with young people already connected to the life of the local church – often the children of parents within the church. 'Outside-in' youth and community work is primarily aimed at those socially distant from the church. Thinking that bridges the two disciplines comes from Green and Christian.[45] They developed the idea of the youth worker 'accompanying' the young person as an example of an overlap between the disciplines of informal education and theology, arguing for the legitimacy of faith-based work. Brierley also blends the two disciplines together. He takes the HMSO definitions of youth work as promoting 'equality of opportunity', 'empowerment', 'participation' and 'education' and then mixes these with the theological ideas of 'Incarnation', 'fellowship', 'worship' and 'mission'. Therefore, youth work and youth ministry, he argues, can take place in and beyond church settings.[46]

At its worst, youth ministry provides a babysitting service for a church that is cash rich and time poor – a safe place where Christian young people can socialize.[47] At its best youth ministry can provide an underpinning structure for a whole strategy of church growth. It develops young people's faith and, at the same time, attracts parents in their thirties and forties. These parents are the age group likely to provide the backbone of church finance and leadership. Churches providing worship for young people are twice as likely to be growing as those not doing so.[48] Soul Survivor, for example, along with its own record label (Worship for a New Generation, www.survivor.co.uk), has been highly effective in providing an event-based programme socializing young people into the Christian faith.

Done badly, youth and community work offers nothing more than a space for young people to hang out and is as likely to reinforce bad habits as to establish good new ones. There has often been an assumed narrative within this type of youth work of young people as disruptive and troublesome, which has been framed round the idea of the dissatisfied adolescent male. Such youth clubs offer young people excluded from mainstream educational provision, snooker or table tennis in case they should get into trouble venting their frustration in other ways.

At its best, however, youth and community work can help to promote a genuine equality of opportunity and support diversity, and is able to recognize and celebrate the differences that exist between individuals whatever their age, sexual orientation, gender, race or disability.

There are limitations to the extent to which both youth and community work and youth ministry are able to introduce young people to the Christian faith in the current context. The informal education endemic to youth and community work is not, by its very nature, going to teach the rubric of the faith. It therefore will not be able to induct young people into the Christian faith. Youth ministry, on the other hand, is able to help those who have already chosen to locate their sense of self within a religious framework, to engage and understand the Christian faith, but it will have little connection with the majority of non-religious youth. Our hope is that an understanding of young people's world view, which unfolds in the next chapters, will help both forms of youth work to connect with young people's spirituality, particularly via the use of popular art and culture.

2

Youth, religion and popular culture

Youth and religion: 'fine, if it works for you'

Does the spirituality in popular culture – aliens, ghosts, demons, angels –
really matter to young people? How important to young people are New Age,
Christian or other world religions? Some theorists have seen the evidence of
religious and spiritual symbolism in popular culture as a cultural turn towards
a postmodern re-enchantment of society, following an extended period of
modern religious decline. Heelas and Woodhead et al., for example, talk about
a spiritual revolution where individual subjective spirituality (transformative
spirituality in our sense) is growing and may even take over from institutional
religion in the future.[1]

But where do young people fit into this? What do we know about young
people's religious beliefs and spiritual sensitivity? What role does popular
culture play?

This chapter provides a brief overview of some of the social science work in
this area. Since research takes some time to process, most of studies in this
chapter refer to Generation X's youth and early Generation Y, who were in
their teens and twenties during the 1980s and 1990s. We conclude the
chapter with a description of the research method we adopted in our study.

Young people's beliefs about religious and spiritual ideas: fuzzy at best

Two things stand out most clearly from recent research conducted in England
and Wales on young people's beliefs. First, young people show a great deal
of fuzziness and uncertainty concerning traditional Christian beliefs.
Yet Christian ideas show a surprising degree of resilience in that they
remain in the *background* of young people's minds. Secondly, Christian and

other religious or spiritual ideas make little real impact on young people's day-to-day living (apart from times of crisis).

Francis's survey of teenagers in England and Wales illustrates this first point very well. Some of his figures are shown in Table 2.1. They indicate that relatively few young people reject belief in God, just 26 per cent compared to 41 per cent who believe and 33 per cent who are not sure.

Table 2.1 Young people's beliefs[2]

	Yes (%)	? (%)	No (%)
I believe in God	41	33	26
I believe that Jesus really rose from the dead	30	42	28
I believe in life after death	45	38	17
I believe God punishes people who do wrong	20	38	42
I believe that God made the world in six days and rested on the seventh	20	40	40
I believe in the Devil	22	28	51

Nearly a third of Francis's young people believed Jesus rose from the dead and nearly half in life after death. Of course, life after death may be conceived of in a number of ways, which may or may not be traditionally Christian. Still, Collins's survey of over a thousand English teenagers found 'heaven' was a widely held belief.[3] Forty-two per cent felt heaven was more than just an imaginary place (although only 22 per cent believed hell was a real place). In the same survey 20 per cent of young people believed in some form of reincarnation after death. These findings suggest traditional Christian beliefs are still around, albeit subject to a degree of selectivity and reinterpretation, which allows young people to give them an individual spin, usually emphasizing the more 'congenial' aspects of the faith. For English youth, God is generally seen as benevolent, if somewhat domesticated. He[4] is more likely to offer comfort than punishment. Indeed, this is one reason why some young people seem to retain religious beliefs: when life goes wrong, God is someone to pray to, something to hold on to. That said, on the whole, the God young people believe in is not a God of awesome power who created the world and performs miracles. Rather, to use Davie's phrase, he is 'an ordinary God':

> Do you believe in God?
>
> Yes.
>
> Do you believe in a God who can change the course of events on earth?
>
> No, just the ordinary one.[5]

Devoid of any real sacred status, this 'God' does not demand to be the source of ultimate meaning and hope for young people. Belief in God is an optional matter, a consumer choice. If belief works for you, fine; if not, drop it.

When young people do reject belief in God, they often do so because they or someone they know has had bad experiences, which undermines their assumption of benevolence – 'experiential atheism' as Richter and Francis call it.[6] Or, they reject belief because they are looking for a more scientific framework to shape their world view, 'philosophical atheism' in Richter and Francis's terms.

More often, young people demonstrate uncertainty about traditional Christian beliefs, rather than rejecting them outright. It may be that this uncertainty reflects a stage in young people's faith development, since typically the teenage years are seen as a period of questioning and pondering some of life's big questions. And this will be the case for some. However, there are other possible explanations for young people's fuzzy uncertainty. First, the religious knowledge of the general culture in which young people are living has declined – modern societies are not good at transmitting the Christian memory from one generation to the next.[7]

We have seen in Chapter 1 that church attendance is in decline. With that we can expect a less thorough socialization into the faith. Levitt's study of Christian mothers supports this view.[8] She found parents were suspicious of churches or schools that were enthusiastic about introducing young people to religion. It is likely that many young people simply do not really know the Christian story well, or do not have the religious language tools to explore them in any depth.[9]

Psychological studies concerning young people's representation of God are a case in point. Janssen, De Hart and Gerardts found that young people in Belgium and Holland referred to God in impersonal, abstract and indefinite terms. A shared, traditional religious language to describe God was simply absent. Churchgoers also described this rather impersonal and abstract God: 'The God of Dutch adolescents is an individual expression of an individual emotion.'[10]

Hutsebaut and Verhoeven also found that most young people in Dutch-speaking Belgium refer to God as a vague (if supernatural) force.[11] It appears from these studies that as traditionally religious language evaporates, personalized, yet vague, explanations flower. Anthropomorphic images of God change to symbolic, abstract and idiosyncratic ones.

A second reason for young people's uncertainty about traditional Christian beliefs is simple indifference! Many young people are happy just to allow for the possibility of a transcendent reality without pursuing it further. This fits with Davie's description of religious beliefs in Europe often being of a 'vicarious', and among the young quite 'precarious', nature.[12] In other words, young people are generally happy for the Church to exist, they are not overtly anti-Church, and indeed even think that it should be there in some form if it helps *others*, for moral reasons or to mark key events in life. However, outside of that they do not want much to do with it themselves.

A third possibility contributing to uncertainty may be that in contemporary society beliefs in themselves are not enough to sustain conviction. Young people also look for experiences to back up their beliefs. As one young Christian described his charismatic experience:

> It [being touched by the Holy Spirit] makes you feel good. It makes you feel, I don't know, wanted – if you see what I mean – because you *know* there is something up there. Before the 'move of the Spirit' everyone *said* there's something up there, so you believe that. But now you *know* that God is there. There's nothing else could have done it.[13]

In this respect we can note the importance of emotional communities for many Christian young people.[14] Interestingly on this point, however, a study of 3,000 Finnish 7- to 20-year-olds indicated that while 80 per cent of children in the 7–11 age range reported having had religious experiences, there is a clear decrease in reported religious experience during puberty around the ages of 13–15 years.[15] From the ages of 15–20, fewer than 10 per cent report frequent religious experience.

Out with the old, in with the new?

You may think that if traditional Christianity is 'old hat', surely the new spirituality on offer in popular culture is a magnet to young people. Not so! Non-church, spiritual ideas also appear vague and attenuated. While 40 per cent of Francis's young people believe in ghosts, only 31 per cent think it is possible to contact spirits. And while 35 per cent say they believe in horoscopes, only 20 per cent believe fortune-tellers can tell the future (see Table 2.2). Furthermore, Heelas and Woodhead et al. found that the more clearly formulated New Age spiritual practices of the holistic milieu tend to attract middle-aged, middle-class women, rather than young people.[16]

Table 2.2 Young people's beliefs about alternative forms of spirituality[17]

	Yes (%)	? (%)	No (%)
I believe in my horoscope	35	29	36
I believe in ghosts	40	29	31
I believe in black magic	20	33	47
I believe that fortune-tellers can tell the future	20	30	50
I believe it is possible to contact the spirits of the dead	31	33	36

These results do not lead us to think many young people are involved in a great deal of spiritual searching (of the transformative type), either inside or outside of institutional religion. Although young people may be willing, even intrigued, to talk about spiritual topics when asked, there appears to be little real evidence of an ongoing 'spiritual quest'.

This is partly due to young people believing themselves to be informed enough already to make their own religious and spiritual choices. On the basis of what their parents tell them and what they learn about religion in school, they feel little need to experiment with different religious or spiritual practices. On the other hand, there is evidence that young people do enjoy the popular arts media that present supernatural ideas.

So what is the relationship between religion and popular culture?

Religion and popular culture

There are three main ways in which we can think about young people using popular art and culture in relation to religion or spirituality. Popular culture is used by a minority of young people with a Christian faith to express their spirituality in church or para-church settings. For another small group of young people, aspects of popular art and culture may take on something of a religious status in their own right. And thirdly, probably for the majority, popular culture can act as a potential means of dialoguing with religious or spiritual ideas.

Popular culture enhancing religion

Popular culture as a means of expressing (transformative) spirituality in churches is not new. Modern styles of worship, particularly since the 1960s, have drawn inspiration from various forms of popular music. There has been a move away from organs and choirs to electronically based worship groups:

the guitars, drums, synthesizers of modern 'choruses'. The Boomer Generation (now grown up) in particular tends to keep within the normal liturgical patterns of the Church, but with more upbeat songs. Beyond this, there has been some very innovative and creative experiments with liturgical practices developed by those working in 'alternative worship'. Alternative worship combines various art forms, including elements of the popular arts, in the liturgy. This combination enables younger people (particularly Generation X young adults in their late twenties and thirties) to celebrate their faith in their own cultural media. For example, Steve Collins describes how music is used within an alternative worship context.

> The music works as a TV or movie-style soundtrack behind everything, or like having music on for background. One thing flowing naturally from another is more important than musical genre, but the DJ soundtrack approach allows a much wider range of music [latin jazz/famous pop anthem/film theme/ symphony] than even the most versatile worship band can supply. The music can comment on what's going on, or change its mood.

> A very large part of the music used is secular stuff brought in from home – because people have perceived spiritual content in it, or just because it works with whatever's going on. The result is that worship has the same soundtrack as the rest of people's lives, but the church context changes the perceived meaning. This can be revelatory, and can stunningly transform the way that the same music is heard in its usual secular context. Some would say that the use of secular music in church profanes church, but the experience of alternative worship is that the current flows the other way![18]

In the United States, Flory and Miller[19] provide detailed ethnographic studies illustrating how some Generation X young people carve out new spaces for religious expression in their existing lifestyle interests, using aspects of the popular arts. For example, they describe the practice of sacred tattooing adopted by groups of young evangelical Christians,[20] and the use of rap and hip hop[21] and street slang in church services.[22]

Popular cultural media can also form an addition to young Christians' more conventional engagements with the Church. One study of online Christian communities, for instance, shows that the Internet is used to form communities that supplement (rather than take over from) the face-to-face relationships of a local church. Subscribers to the e-community found a degree of support and like-mindedness which was sometimes lacking for them in the local church.[23] It is likely that this will be a means of relating to the world that will have increasing relevance for Generation Y young Christians in the future. For young Christians then, the popular arts can be an important way of engaging with the faith and developing transformative spirituality.

Popular culture 'as' religion

Some theorists have argued that outside of the Christian Church popular culture can take on religious or spiritual significance in its own right. In other words, some aspects of popular culture can potentially become forms of 'invisible' or 'implicit' religion. As discussed in Chapter 1, the idea of 'invisible' religion suggests that any set of practices or beliefs that bind people together into a community and help people make sense of themselves and their lives can be understood as 'religious'. The classic example of popular culture as religion pertains to sport 'as religion' – for example football in Britain or baseball in the United States.[24] In this respect, sports offer the potential for personal transformation, such as transcending the normal limitations of the body. Sports also provide a basis for community, identity and history. Sports can be said to have their own liturgy with rituals and ceremonies and foci for devotion in the form of top sportsmen and women. Aside from sports, the imaginary worlds and ideologies conjured up in the popular arts through books, television programmes and films also have the potential to be appropriated by audiences. A minority will even turn them into the basis of a quasi-religious movement. *Star Trek* fan-dom is one such example.[25]

Parallels can easily be drawn between these forms of popular culture and religion. However, it is important to keep in mind that parallels do not necessarily mean complete likeness. As Higgs argues, 'Sports are like religion in many ways just as they are like war in some ways, but they are not equatable with either.'[26]

Perhaps there is a greater case for seeing rave, and club culture more generally, as a potentially religious or spiritual phenomenon in so far as it is heavily infused with overtly religious symbolism. During a rave at its most sophisticated, the trance states induced by dance, techno-music and drugs have much in common with religious experiences.[27] (Indeed, rave culture has been an inspiration of some aspects of alternative worship.) This is a theme we explore in more detail in Chapter 5.

Resourcing religion through popular culture

This leaves us with the idea of popular culture as a resource for religious and spiritual ideas. In this sense, young people can use popular culture to inform and shape their own world view and spirituality. This is the central concern of our study.

The potential for popular culture to be used as a resource has been regarded with ambivalence by certain sections of the Christian constituency. On the one hand, there is a tradition of using popular culture, especially the mass media, to promote the Christian faith. Aside from the most obvious forms of TV evangelism, in the United States the Evangelical Church has developed a whole Christian entertainment industry that include films such as *A Thief in the Night* (1973), *The Omega Code* (1999) and *Left Behind: The Movie* (2001), which are designed to encourage people to turn to Christ.[28] *The Miracle Maker* (2000) animation film and Mel Gibson's *The Passion of Christ* (2004) have both been shown in Britain recently, and both have been used by Christian groups for evangelistic purposes.

At the same time, some conservative Christian groups have been wary about the potential of popular culture to corrupt young people and lead them 'astray' (as they see it). Popular culture can be perceived as introducing alternative, possibly even dangerous, religious ideas and supernatural practices. For example, the *Harry Potter* and *Lord of the Rings* books and films have been seen by some as soft-peddling occultic ideas,[29] and conservative parents have steered their children away from them. Undoubtedly, young people's greatest access to ideas about magic and other supernatural ideas outside of institutional religion is through television programmes, films, magazines, books and tabloid newspapers.

However, the true extent of popular culture's ability to persuade young people about religious or spiritual ideas of whatever kind is unclear. In Collins's[30] survey of English teenagers, 21 per cent indicated that television and radio influenced their religious beliefs. Nye[31] found children in her research referred to the soap opera *Neighbours* as a source of knowledge and belief in reincarnation (although not Hinduism or other more general belief systems). Francis[32] found that those young people who watched more than 4 hours of television a day were less likely to believe in God or that Jesus rose from the dead, and more likely to believe in horoscopes, ghosts, black magic, fortune-telling and spiritualism than those who watched less television.

In contrast, Clark's detailed analysis of American teenagers' relationship with the supernatural through film and television tells a different story.[33] Clark's work indicates that generally American young people are not, primarily at least, persuaded by media representations of the supernatural (e.g. angels, the occult, aliens), although they do sometimes find it fun to play with the ideas. In her sample of 102 teenagers, Clark identified five groups of American young people according to their reactions to spiritual ideas in television programmes:

- 'Resisters' dismissed organized religion as being unscientific, but liked to think about the supernatural in so far as it could be interpreted in a quasi-scientific way. Thus God could be an alien for these young people, and they enjoyed programmes with alien themes.

- 'Mystical' teens were those young people who did not practise any organized religion but were open to beliefs in the supernatural primarily because it was fun to think about. Where they did engage more fully with supernatural ideas they mainly understood them through the framework of cultural Christianity. In other words, Christianity was the baseline from which to interpret popular culture rather than popular culture leading them away from the Church.

- 'Experimenters' were young people who had a prior religious commitment and wanted to engage more fully with the supernatural realm. Clark indicates that of all the young people she interviewed these teenagers came closest to 'seeker' status. However, they were generally seeking a connection with the supernatural *within* their existing religious tradition, not outside of it. Popular culture did not persuade them to take on a different religion or take up occult practices.

- 'Traditionalists' were religiously committed young people. On the whole they did not engage with the alternative forms of the supernatural as mediated through popular culture.

- Finally Clark refers to the 'Intrigued' teenagers who were religiously committed but were interested by the supernatural realm.

Following her description of each of these groups of American young people, Clark came to five conclusions relevant to our study. First, young people primarily related to the supernatural in popular culture for its *entertainment value*. On the whole this meant they were not taken seriously. Even the Intrigued group understood the supernatural in this context as fantasy. Consequently Clark states:

> I wouldn't predict that many young people will decide to convert to Wiccan or neo-Pagan religions because of their interest in what they have seen in the television program *Charmed* or the Harry Potter films, among other such stories.[34]

27

Secondly, although (or perhaps because) the supernatural in this context was largely inconsequential, the young people did not want to close down on ideas about the supernatural. They wanted to retain the possibility of there being something beyond the material world. On the rare occasions when young people might need it, the supernatural offered a possible means of making sense of immediate circumstances. However, Collins[35] found that among English youth such 'emergency' meaning making is unlikely to extend to a permanent belief framework.

Thirdly, young people did not approach media representations of the supernatural in a vacuum. Personal experience of institutional religion (however minimal), the influences of their peers and parents, and their socio-economic, racial and gendered identity impinge. Interestingly, it was those young people whose parents had experimented with seances, Ouija boards, and the like, who were most likely to explore these areas themselves. Religious engagement, or lack of it, was not usually a form of rebellion against parental culture but rather an extension of it.

Fourthly, young people who were not particularly involved in religion or engaging with the supernatural, but who nevertheless claimed a religious or spiritual identity, did so mainly because being religious or spiritual was associated with being a good and moral person. The young people did not want to see themselves as people devoid of moral worth.

Finally, both young people's engagement with the supernatural, and the media representations of the supernatural, placed a heavy emphasis on individualism. The supernatural relates, for good or ill, to individuals rather than groups or society. In this respect, when the young people did relate to supernatural ideas they did so through the American culture of individualism.

The religious climate of the United States is, of course, very different from that in Britain. While the exact figures are disputed, many more people in the United States attend church and see religion as a significant part of their lives than in Britain. Nevertheless, Clark's study provides a useful comparison point for our work. In Chapter 3, we will set out how English youth both compare and contrast with American young people.

Young people using popular culture

The American young people in Clark's study demonstrated a high degree of sophistication when it came to reading popular culture. It is well established that young people in the West are media savvy and, far from being passive consumers of whatever is delivered to them, they are active and creative in their interpretation of symbols and messages. In other words, there is a bottom-up relationship as well as a top-down one with popular culture. Paul Willis's work is important in this respect. He demonstrated how young people in the 1980s engaged in an ongoing process of symbolic creativity as they related to popular culture. He argued that while the popular cultural industries might try to send young people one type of message, young people themselves may well construct, and therefore receive, another: 'The fundamental point is that "messages" are not now so much "sent" and "received" as *made* in reception, often as a result of, or at least appearing in the space made free and usable by the operation of grounded aesthetics.'[36]

One example of young people's active relationship to popular culture is their relationship to television adverts. Willis described how young people could consume commercials independently of the products they advertise. Young people enjoyed the creative process of exploring the relationship between images, words and meaning which advertisers brought together. As individuals and in groups, young people were also found to take pleasure in evaluating and criticizing an advert's production quality, sometimes arguing that television adverts were better than the main programmes, or at least more enjoyable, because they allowed the young people to engage in this creative symbolic work.

Popular culture also enables young people to form and express aspects of their personal and social identity. Miles suggests that popular culture offers the tools through which young people can construct lifestyles, articulating their individuality as well as their social belonging.[37] A lifestyle allows the expression of individuality though a person's patterns of leisure and consumption. Lifestyles are, to some degree at least, open to individual choice and taste. They also express social belonging because they are shared with others, and the values they imbibe are socially derived. Miles argues that 'lifestyle' is a more appropriate concept for the analysis of contemporary youth's relationship with culture than the old idea of youth subcultures. This is because the focus is no longer on the idea of subversive youth (which dominated the sociology of youth during the 1970s and 1980s). Miles suggests the majority of young people today, Generation Y, are not challenging the normative order of consumer capitalism. Rather, they accept it, even if they cannot fully participate in it. Moreover, when employment and other traditional means of identity formation are unpredictable, leisure and lifestyle pursued through popular culture take on more importance in the construction of identity:

> The modern significance of a lifestyle may arise as a solution to
> the existential problems of boredom, meaninglessness, and lack
> of control, problems created by the confluence of affluence and
> the destruction of the traditional centers of meaning, religion,
> work, family, and the community.[38]

This is not to say, of course, that ethnicity, gender or class no longer matter. These factors clearly continue to influence what lifestyles are deemed appropriate, valuable and available. It is to say, however, that an understanding of young people's *uses of popular culture* is central to understanding their world view and potentially their spirituality. We took this as a starting point when we analysed our data.

In the next chapter (Chapter 3), we present an overview of the research findings. We consider from our own research whether, as Greeley suggests, people can find in popular culture 'a locale in which to encounter God'.[39]

How we went about doing this is set out below.

Research method

The scope of our project was potentially huge. Popular culture includes a wide range of art forms. In order to keep our study to a manageable size, we had to be selective about what we covered. Tom Wright's analysis of world views provided us with a helpful framework within which to make our choices. Wright suggests world views are expressed through *story, symbol* and *praxis*. For Wright, stories are 'the most characteristic expression of [a] worldview, going deeper than isolated observation or fragmented remark'.[40] Stories address fundamental existential questions such as those mentioned in Chapter 1: 'Who are we?', 'Where are we?', 'What is wrong [with the world]?', 'What is the solution?'[41] and 'What time is it?' or 'Where are we in the story?'[42] Stories run deep in the collective consciousness and are powerful because they engage with all aspects of the human psyche – rationality, imagination and emotion. The stories of world views are expressed through cultural symbols. These include images, artefacts and events. As well as reminding us of the world view and making it visible, symbols can mark out social boundaries – in so far as those who observe them are 'insiders' and those who do not are 'outsiders'. World views are also expressed through praxis, 'a-way-of-being-in-the-world'.[43] What we do, how we act and how we spend our time express our values and priorities. Wright illustrates the interaction between these dimensions as shown in Figure 2.1 opposite.[44]

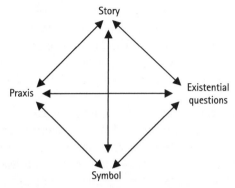

Figure 2.1 Interaction between story, symbol, praxis and existential questions.

Given this framework, we decided to concentrate on forms of popular culture which epitomized each dimension and which had wide appeal to young people. We could then see what young people made of them in constructing their own world views. For story, we chose to concentrate on films and television soap operas. We felt that films offered an overarching narrative that the interviewees could relate to or reject, whereas soap operas were more focused and concerned with the ongoing details of local relationships. For symbol, we decided to concentrate on young people's reactions to advertising images and cultural icons. We felt praxis would best be reflected in popular music and clubbing. Our choice of popular cultural forms can be mapped on to Wright's dimensions as shown in Figure 2.2.

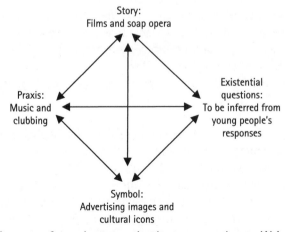

Figure 2.2 Aspects of popular art and culture mapped onto Wright's dimensions.

Using our framework, we conducted a series of 25 semi-structured group interviews with young people, around each of the three areas, and carried out some observations of nightclubs. Group interviews were chosen as our primary method because they offered a flexible way of getting rich qualitative data that would reflect the shared, social nature of world views.

During the interviews, we encouraged our interviewees to speak freely among themselves in response to some general 'prompt' questions and stimuli, which we provided. As far as possible, we let the conversation flow naturally, probing as appropriate in response to the comments the interviewees made. This provided rich, spontaneous data for a grounded, bottom-up approach to our analysis. At the same time, the semi-structured approach allowed us to include a few questions that were more specifically directed towards our purposes. These 'task questions' were incorporated when the natural flow of the conversation allowed, and facilitated some top-down analysis across the different groups.

The interviews were structured around our three strands of story, praxis and symbol. It was not always possible to cover all of the three strands, but there was usually time for at least two. The ordering of the strands was varied between groups.

Story: TV soaps and films

Most of the interviews began with story. We encouraged the interviewees to speak freely about their viewing habits in relation to soap operas and films. The interviewees were asked if they watched *EastEnders* and, if so, what storyline came to mind, and which characters appealed to them most. The interviewees generally found no difficulty in responding to these questions and elaborated on their ideas as the discussion developed. The task question in relation to soap storylines was, 'What would you do if you were in that situation?'

Just as we encouraged the interviewees to speak freely about soaps, we also asked them to comment on their favourite films, or on films they had recently seen. For comparative purposes, the interviewees were also asked directly about one or more of the following films (if they had not already been mentioned in the course of that discussion): *Lord of the Rings: The Fellowship of the Ring, Harry Potter: The Philosopher's Stone, The Blair Witch Project, The Matrix, Star Wars* and *Terminator 2.* These films were chosen because the interviewees were likely to have seen them and because they suggested a connection with a meaningful reality beyond the material world. Our rationale was that if the interviewees' world views did reference a reality transcending their experience of day-to-day life, or indicated a search for meaning beyond the here and now, this would be reflected in their comments about these films.

Praxis: Music and clubbing

The praxis strand of our group interviews concentrated on music and clubbing. By way of stimuli we played five music tracks. Our selection, following the advice of two young DJs, reflected a range of styles that would be current for young people. These were: Iio's 'Rapture' (dance), Mary J. Blige's 'Family Affair' (R&B), The Streets' 'Pure Garage' (garage), Afroman's 'Because I Got High' (garage) and Faithless' 'Drifting Away' (house). The interviewees listened to 60 seconds of each track and were asked in an open-ended manner for their thoughts and feelings towards each one in turn. The task part of this strand was a series of follow-up questions relating to clubbing: 'What is the best thing about clubbing?', 'What is the worst thing about clubbing?', 'Have you ever experienced anything out of the ordinary while clubbing?', 'Do you carry over anything of what you experience in clubbing to your everyday life?'

Symbol: Cultural icons and adverts

With symbol we presented the interviewees with 15 different images and asked for their thoughts and feelings in response to them. The images were carefully chosen to reflect something of Wright's existential questions and are described in Chapter 6. The task question in this strand of the group interviews involved asking the interviewees to choose an image to which they could particularly relate and then to explain their choice. Two of the group interviews also included a grouping exercise whereby the interviewees were asked to choose three or four images and group them around a story of their own making. Again the interviewees were asked to explain their choice.

Each group interview lasted between one and two hours. With the permission of the interviewees, all of the sessions were audio-recorded and then transcribed in full.

The young people who took part

The young people were recruited for group interviews through youth clubs, universities and colleges we had contact with. A total of 124 young people in our preferred age range of 15- to 25-years took part in our study. The group interviews were spread over 18 sites countrywide.[45] Eighteen of the interviews were held in youth club settings, six in universities and two in colleges. The size of the groups varied. Twenty-three groups had between two and nine young people, two were larger.[46] Nineteen of the groups were mixed; four were males only and three females only. Just over half of the interviewees were female (52 per cent) and the majority (94 per cent) were White (the remainder including both Black and Asian young people), reflecting some of the main demographic characteristics of English youth. Some 60 per cent of the young people defined themselves as non-Christian and 40 per cent as Christian.

In addition to the group interviews we also included some observation as part of our data collection on music and clubbing. We attended two well-known London nightclubs in order to observe and gain a taste of young people's clubbing experience. On both occasions, field notes were written up directly after the visits to record both behavioural observations and the essence of conversations with clubbers.

The transcripts from the interviews and our observational field notes were coded for themes and analysed using a qualitative computer software package.[47] To test whether our analysis fitted well with young people's own understandings of the world, we presented our interpretation to two 'expert witnesses' – two 18-year-old male DJs who had their fingers very much on the pulse of youth culture. In the course of a two-hour discussion, these DJs confirmed our conclusions.

The next chapter sets out our general findings and describes what we believe to be the world view of the Generation Y young people who took part in our study.

3

Our findings: The Happy midi-narrative

We were impressed by the creativity with which our young people engaged with our chosen elements of popular culture. They used films, television soap operas, popular music, clubbing, cultural icons and advertising images for their *own purposes*: to resource a world view in which happiness for themselves, their friends, and their families is the bedrock. The logic of this is simply self-evident:

> Happiness is the ideal you aim for. (Derek)

Below we set out our findings in more detail, but we begin with two caveats. The first is to restate the nature of our sample: our interviewees were 'socially included' young people. Gossiping with friends about *EastEnders*, downloading music, a night's clubbing, going to the cinema all require access to televisions, texting, emailing, Internet, CD players, iPods, and above all, cash. Even though the price of technology is coming down all the time, the financial outlay can still be considerable. Furthermore, our young people attended a youth club, college or university. Therefore generalizations to other young people on the margins of society are inappropriate, at least at this stage. That said, 'included' young people constitute the majority of youth. It is important to hear their voice.

Our second caveat is a reminder that our data, gathered primarily through group interviews, is *social* data. We have tapped into a socially shared (and socially acceptable) world view arising between young people through their interactions with the popular arts. The popular arts, consumed communally and discussed in groups, provided our young people with valued 'cultural capital' and shared experiences, thus creating something of a sense of community:

> I think the appeal of things like *Big Brother* and *Pop Idol* and

that, is that it's conversation, isn't it? You go out and you say: 'Oh my God, did you see *Pop Idol?* Did you see what Will did? Did you see what Gareth did?' And it's something to talk about, and it's something that's in the news all the time. And you feel like you're missing out [if you don't know what's going on]. It's like Gareth is on the front cover [of the papers] crying his eyes out or something, you are like 'Oh my God, what happened?' you know. (Helen)

We do not claim that the world view we present here is fully comprehensive. Socially constructed world views interact with personal experiences and ideas. A young person's individual outlook on life may involve a host of other influences (parents, school, work, friends), involving pains or joys not articulated here. Yet, given the density of social interaction among young people, which to a large degree revolves around communal consumption of the popular arts, we believe the world view we have uncovered has power precisely *because* it is socially shared and socially acceptable. It is a world view that the young people present, not just to us as researchers, but to each other as well.

A secularized world view

We fished with our best lures. We presented young people with a range of examples from the popular arts which we thought could provoke comments which at least hinted at a reality beyond the immediate, material world – that is, if the young people were inclined to use such ideas. We were particularly interested in their spontaneous use of, or reference to, religious, spiritual or supernatural concepts. Rather than coercing such ideas with direct questions, we presented 'lures'. We believed that this indirect approach would most closely approximate how young people normally respond to and interpret the art forms and the world around them.

However, we did not find much evidence of any such ideas coming to the fore. Traditional religious concepts and stories did not seem to have much relevance at all. They did not seem to constitute part of the young people's natural frame of reference in the way that they appear to have done for Clark's[1] teenagers in the United States (see Chapter 2). For example, in our pilot interviews we included a picture of Salvador Dali's *Christ of St John of the Cross* (1951). We had to drop it from the main interviews because the young people failed to respond to it in any significant way. ('Oh, my grandmother has that picture', was one such response).

Similarly, other images with traditionally religious connotations failed to have much resonance with the young people (see Chapter 6). Discussions of the moral issues represented in soap operas and films indicated that ethical judgements did not rely on a conscious connection with the traditional religious rationales of right and wrong (Chapter 4). Neither did we find much evidence among our young people of beliefs in other spiritual or supernatural realms beyond the here and now. Discussions around *Buffy the Vampire Slayer*, for example, did not open out into talk about alternative spiritual realities; and young people's experiences of clubbing were generally well rooted in the tangible experiences of a night out, rather than being seen as a way of transcending oneself and touching a deeper reality (see Chapter 5). Discussion of the events surrounding September 11th failed to elicit mention of religion (or even religious conflict) (Chapter 6). In all these respects, therefore, the world view we found among our young people was secularized in the sense that any institutionally based religious awareness, or ideas of a spiritual or supernatural reality, were not given much salience or social significance.

Our findings fit with the previous research set out in Chapters 1 and 2, which suggests that young people's stock of traditional religious knowledge and levels of religious engagement are very limited indeed. However, lack of overt religious sensibility did not appear to result in our young people feeling disenchanted, alienated or lost in a meaningless world. Instead, the data indicated that they found meaning and significance in the reality of everyday life, which the popular arts helped them to understand and imbibe. In this respect, we believe we found a coherent narrative that underpins our young people's world view. In essence, it states: 'This world, and all life in it, is meaningful *as it is.*' In other words, there is no need to posit ultimate significance elsewhere beyond the immediate experience of everyday life. This means that our young people had no obvious need for what we call transformative spirituality (Chapter 1). If youth workers are looking for a felt need, a 'God-shaped hole' that follows Christian contours, they will be disappointed. We did find, however, that a basic, formative spirituality ran through much of young people's engagement with the world (see Part Two).

The Happy midi-narrative

We have coined the phrase 'Happy midi-narrative' to describe the storyline of our young people's world view. We use the term 'midi-narrative' to distinguish it from the concept of a 'meta-narrative'. A meta-narrative is a story on a grand scale about how the world works. Meta-narratives are often stories with an end goal. For example, in the Enlightenment meta-narrative the goal is 'progress' and the improvement of the human condition. In the Judaeo-Christian meta-narrative, we could say that the goal is the 'end times', the return of the Messiah. In contrast, the world view of our young people operates on a more modest scale of the here and now, rather than something beyond. Yet it is not an individualistic, mini-narrative. It is communal on a small scale (me, my friends, and my family): a midi-narrative.

'Happy' refers to the fact that central to our young people's world view is the belief that the universe and social world are essentially benign and life is OK. Of course, the young people recognized that difficult things happen (broken relationships, rape, divorce, violence); indeed, they had experienced some of these things themselves. But they also evidenced a belief that there are enough resources within the individual and his or her family and friends to enable happiness to prevail. There was no need to explain why happiness is the goal of life – this was self-evident to our young people.

Within the Happy midi-narrative, we could discern different levels of happiness. At the deep end, it entails joy, ecstasy, elation, well-being and a sense of shared bliss. The potential for a relationally conceived formative spirituality can be glimpsed here: a spirituality for this world, rather than for a future heaven. There is a self-actualizing aspect to this happiness, but the essence of the deep end is more relational than individualistic. The shallow end of the Happy midi-narrative evokes the meaning of the phrase 'happy-go-lucky': carefree, light-hearted, escapist, nonchalant, untroubled. Interestingly, while we as researchers might want to make much of this distinction, the shallow and deep ends are not viewed by the young people as mutually exclusive, or even one judged as better than the other. Thus deep happiness is not threatened by the shallow happiness that comes with, say, getting 'off your head' in a club.

Shallow happiness can lead into deep happiness, and vice versa, as both are made of the same 'stuff': human beings in relationship with each other. Through human relationships and having fun, happiness can be achieved. This matters more than which sort of happy feeling is promoted. Both the deep and shallow ends of the Happy midi-narrative[2] are present, seamlessly in the data, gaining equal approbation. To posit a 'new Jerusalem coming down from heaven' at the end of time is simply not necessary.

On the basis of our data, we were able to flesh out a fuller rendition of the Happy midi-narrative using a three-part sequence typical of basic stories such as folk tales.[3] This is our composite expression of the ideas implicit and explicit in the young people's comments during the interviews. It is not an ideology spelt out by any particular individuals, yet it seems to summarize and give form to the perspective from which the young people were operating:

1. **Initial sequence of main storyline.** 'My aim to be happy will be realized through me being myself, and connecting to others and the universe (without harming them). As I do this, I will create a meaningful and happy life. If we all make this individual effort (everyone's own responsibility), each person's happiness will sum into a corporate experience of unity and enjoyment. This happiness is meaningful in itself; it is the Ideal.'

2. **Topical sequence: The obstacle and the help.** 'Bad things can happen in real life that prevent us from attaining this happiness: broken relationships, suffering, loneliness, depression, self-rejection, addiction, injustice, ageing. But each one of us is surrounded by resources of family and close friends who love us unconditionally. The popular arts provide us with valuable resources: information, choice, creativity. With these, we can experience movement from the Actual (real life where bad things can happen) towards the Ideal (happiness).'

3. **Final sequence: The resolution.** 'Having received help, having "grown" as a result of the meaningful microcosm of family, friends and the popular arts, the happy Ideal that once eluded us is now possible.'

The Happy midi-narrative and popular culture are in something of a dialectical relationship in that each informs the other. Our young people brought the Happy midi-narrative to their reading and evaluation of popular arts storylines in films, television soaps and song lyrics. The life of singer Mary J. Blige, for example, fitted the narrative neatly. Although she was a successful singer, and therefore should have been living out the Happy midi-narrative, she was defeated by drugs and alcohol. Yet she overcame that stage of her life and her latest songs are happier. When one of her songs was played during the focus groups, the interviewees liked her, identified with her and found her music meaningful. While most other music was considered simply as 'accompaniment to mood', Mary J. Blige told a story they could believe in (see Chapter 5). Similarly, films in which the central character faced and overcame obstacles were celebrated as long as they were seen to be 'realistic' and provided reliable information about the real world (see Chapter 4). *EastEnders*, on the other hand, was often considered frustrating or false, when its characters failed to utilize the resources available to them to overcome their problems, or when life was portrayed by the programme as unremittingly bleak.

Bob (interviewer):	Why don't you like it [*EastEnders*]?
Lucy:	Because it's not true to life at all.
Jez:	No, not at all. No one goes through their life like that. All of it [*EastEnders*] is all woe, it's all sorrow.

Equally, popular culture helped the young people to interpret their actual, lived world (henceforth called the Actual) and to imagine and experience something of their ideal world (the Ideal), and provide a bridge between the two.

The Actual

The young people's actual world was perceived as largely benign, if sometimes a little dull. While bad things do happen in real life, and people have weaknesses and failings, problems were seen as solvable through self-reliance, family and friends. In this respect kinship (i.e. blood relations) took precedence over other types of relations, confirming the local nature of this midi-narrative world view. Indeed, the young people felt there was something of a normative moral obligation on family members to help each other, whether or not this reflected their personal family experience.

The Ideal

The ideal world could be glimpsed through the popular arts since they provided the tools of imagination and a taste of experience. Alongside happiness, this ideal world for our young people is marked by excitement, action, promise – the Ideal is a place where the young people could fully be themselves. In other words, the Ideal is a happier, more vital version of their actual lived reality. Advertisements such as the Levi's commercial of two youths running through walls, along felled trees and leaping over a great chasm evoked this sense of hope:[4]

> Advertising is like such an important thing, it, like, drives us so much. It's like at the moment we have this Levi advert on TV . . . it is such a good advert . . . it catches some sort of longing for stuff to be, like, something different and, like, a kind of sense of

freedom and it's ridiculous how much that advert has affected our lives. Everywhere we go we will comment on the advert if we see it . . . Anyway advertising really, really drives me on what I do in life generally, I know that's really sad but it's actually true, advertising really affects what I think, what I do, what I buy, yep! (Diana)

The ideal self for both our young men and women was strong and in control of his or her life, good looking and surrounded by supportive family and friends. There was no need to be a victim. Linked to this there is an ethical code that stipulates the virtue of tolerance. People should try to find their happy ideal in whatever way they can, provided they do not prevent the happiness of others (particularly family and friends). In this respect, the self is not set against 'the other'. Efforts devoted to oneself to realize one's own potential, to enhance one's attractiveness, to have a good time, need not be at the expense of others. 'She's always up for it' is a compliment paid to those who party hard, evoking a sort of new work ethic, which at the shallow end, upholds the Happy midi-narrative for the good of all.

In contrast to the dichotomies prevailing in church culture, young people do not suffer from the dualism that elevates intellectual knowing over emotional, experiential knowing. They did not speak of the Ideal in abstract, disembodied terms, but rather approached it through their experiences. In the ideal world people feel good about themselves and life – they are happy. How one *feels* is decisive and is a dominant strain in young people's moral reasoning. Truth is not considered to be abstract and 'out there', but personal and pragmatic.

Popular arts mediating between the Actual and Ideal

The different popular arts we used seemed to mediate between young people's experience of the Actual and Ideal in particular ways. Some popular arts offered more experience of the Actual (real life), and some provided more of a doorway to the Ideal, how they would like life to be.

Visual images (cultural icons and adverts) enable young people to examine and articulate what life is actually like. Television soaps also enable young people to focus on the Actual, and afford some information for problem solving, providing a transforming bridge that enables young people to inch towards the happy Ideal. In this respect, popular arts provide a rehearsal space to engage with the complexity of life in a manageable way. Thus, the popular arts need to be 'realistic' in order to facilitate problem solving, learning from other's mistakes, identifying with others and their situations, emotional catharsis and *schadenfreude* ('I feel better now that I know others are worse off than me'). Soaps can also serve as pure 'entertainment', an escape to the shallow end.

Films (watched in cinemas) hover more closely towards the Ideal, giving an experience of a large-scale exciting, creative, alternative reality. Clubbing has the potential to 'incarnate' the ideal Happy midi-narrative; it is both a symbol and praxis. Music, ubiquitous in our young people's lives, pervades the entire world view. It is the soundtrack for both the Actual and the Ideal, accompanying rather than commanding. Music provides the vehicle for emotion and identity, for feeling and experiencing life in all its variety (see Chapter 5).

Only getting 'stuck' seemed to threaten happiness, and the emergence of the Ideal. As long as there is movement, there is hope. And so the concept of 'edge' requires that the popular arts stay sharp, novel, ever carving out new territory. Together, then, the popular arts offer the wherewithal for our young people to move back and forth in their experience of the Actual and the Ideal, as represented in Figure 3.1. The centre of the figure represents the Ideal, and the outside, the Actual. The arrows indicate the two-way travel between the Actual and Ideal.

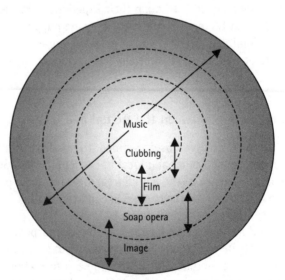

Figure 3.1 Popular culture's relationship to the Actual and Ideal.

Absent from the Happy midi-narrative

Certain themes and concerns that might have been expected in the context of the group discussions were conspicuously absent from the emerging storyline. Most significant of these are: God and sin, fear of death, romance and sexual fulfilment, achievement, and structural inequalities.

God

As we have already mentioned above, the young people responded in a rather flat way to overtly religious representations in the popular arts we used. For example,

> *Image: Benetton ad: Man dying of AIDS*
>
> Bob (interviewer): They have put the face of Jesus on someone dying of AIDS.
>
> Simon: But still, I don't care about that.

Sin

No concept for sin (as moral transgression or moral degradation) or salvation from sin was apparent. Nor did the interviewees appear to be experiencing anxiety or guilt as a result of a 'Freudian' struggle between repressive social norms and private sensual desires.[5] In a similar vein, it does not appear to be necessary for young people to rebel against their parents. In fact, much is held in common with them: for example, *EastEnders* appeals to and is enjoyed by both.

Fear of death

Death is perceived as less problematic than ageing, which is attended by depression. For young people, of course, death is far away and not a relevant concern, while the potential unattractiveness and loneliness of ageing are real threats. While death did not evoke existential questioning, communal and religious rituals surrounding death were to be respected if these are helpful in providing meaning and continuity for the living.

Romance and sexual fulfilment

In both single-sex and mixed group interviews, romantic partnerships appeared to be viewed as peripheral or problematic. This may reflect the relative youth and inexperience of our interviewees, and the constraints that group interviews place on the expression of private emotion. It seems also to reflect young people's awareness that romantic relationships take work: one needs to be attractive, to be skilled in relationships and in sex. Relationships are seen as inherently risky – they often end in disaster. Break-ups, jealousy, adultery, divorce, HIV are ever-present pitfalls.

Image: Charles and Diana's wedding

> It just shows that people can think they are so in love and everything ... but then things can change [and it is] all swept away. (Tanya)

Instead, interviewees showed a fervent faith in the family as a source of unconditional support, despite statistical and real-life evidence to the contrary. While romantic relationships are desired, they are not seen to provide the resources for young people to solve their problems.

It might be supposed that the diminished importance of romantic storylines indicates greater gender equality, yet our data does not entirely support this. While females are expected to be strong, they are also *required* to be attractive from a male point of view (see Chapters 4 and 6).

Achievement

Although admired in stars, material success and grand-scale achievement are not central to our young people's world view. Happiness is seen as relationally based.

Structural inequalities

Racism did not arise as an issue. Our young people showed no evidence of being racist, yet there appeared to be no great desire to be inclusive. Personal choice is overestimated as constituting the differences between social groups. Being discriminating and selective is the significant indicator of who you are.

Music: R&B track

Jill:	I like it and I'm not Black am I.
Richard:	No it's not ... it's not a colour thing at all ...
Karen:	Then why is it a cultural thing?
Richard:	It's the culture they have grown up in ...

Inevitably, less time is available for wider issues of collective identity such as political or racial questions. Life is lived out on a constantly changing 'midi' scale.

Themes present in the Happy midi-narrative

While some themes were conspicuously absent from the storyline, other core themes emerged, notably life, the family (as a symbol of security), celebrities and commercialism.

Life

While our young people rarely spoke about God or a transcendent realm, they are not mere materialist hedonists. They care deeply about life, symbolized in newborns, children, the planet, animals. Life is an ultimate value, and a key to young peoples' moral reasoning, which has a strong emotional component (discussed in Chapter 4 and 6).

Image: Newborn

Zach: It's an amazing moment seeing a newborn baby. And although she is screaming out into the breadth of life I think it's just, you know, an amazing sense of the fragility of life and also the beauty of life.

Jason: Yes, the first, like, few moments of a person's life makes you wonder what, who they are now.

Image: David Bailey's anti-fur advert

Frankie: Dumb animals.

Natasha: Oh that's horrible.

Nigel: That just makes you think about not wearing fur.

Natasha: I can't do that anyway.

Frankie: I hate animal cruelty.

Natasha: Yeah.

Frankie: I love animals so much and that makes me feel sick.

Family

Family is an unquestioned absolute and symbol of security: 'Family are there for you.'

Image: Man dying of AIDS

... united in the fact that if you are going to be ill you know your family is going to be there to support you regardless of colour, race, gender, whatever; the family is going to be there to support you. (Helen)

The data shows that identity formation ('Who am I?') is firmly located within the network of family and friends. Our young people showed a *faith* in family and in their own agency. The idea (perhaps more than the reality) of family is seen to provide young people with a sense of ultimate security, even in the face of death.

If you are dying, you want your family around you. (Nigel)

Image: Man dying of AIDS

Yes, sad, it would be sad, but the family is there to support him which is very comforting. (Helen)

Intergenerational 'vertical' ties form the stable warp, while horizontal ties (e.g. lovers, partners, spouses) provide the flexible woof in young people's network of relationships. While much uncertainty attends the horizontal relationships within families (due to divorce, re-marriage, cohabitation, combined step-families), the roles between generations are clearly defined, and it is the function of these intergenerational 'blood' relationships to provide security.

Celebrities

Celebrities such as pop stars, movie stars, supermodels and athletes seem to enjoy creative, well-paid work which allows them potentially to live the Happy midi-narrative full-time. In the unstinting media coverage of these people, echoes of the Happy midi-narrative are continuously heard. Celebrities often assert in media interviews that they are 'happy with their lives' (be that following a third divorce, box office success or drug rehabilitation), and that is an assertion which fends off criticism. In our data, celebrities (such as Madonna, Posh and Becks) define and embody social categories such as gender. They tell young people what they should or should not be like.

Image: Madonna

Joanna: She is such a beautiful person, like, outwards and

> inwards. That was kind of her stage where she was trying to, like, impress a lot more than she is now; but now she is, like, much more calmer and she is still really beautiful.

Bob: So you say she is beautiful outwards as well as inwards. Do you agree with that?

Linda: I agree with that, yeah.

Bob: Is she quite a good role model or . . .

Joanna: I think she is a good role model.

Linda: She is now, yeah.

Popular culture is dependent upon the making and unmaking of stars, and these processes are of continual interest to young people. Reality television such as *Big Brother, Survivor, Pop Idol*, which make and unmake celebrities (thus making stardom accessible to the ordinary person) were very popular with our young people. There is an ambivalence here: popular culture extols our stars, and then seeks to topple them. This too upholds the Happy midi-narrative, as no one person has a monopoly on attention, and there is room for the ordinary person at the top. This keeps the panoply of the gods moving, and movement keeps the hope alive.

Commercialism

While music in particular symbolizes creativity, choice and identity, whenever a product becomes 'too commercial' (an oft-repeated judgement) whatever value it once had is destroyed. In the eyes of our young people, the popular arts have to maintain 'edge'. Yet edge is undermined by commercial success. A deep tension is felt by young people about the Shiva-like nature of consumer capitalism that both enables and destroys the life world. While the market enables valued choice and autonomy, it also destroys creativity and independence through commercialism.

> They were edge but now they are commercial. (Nigel)

Basic questions

From the storyline, symbols and practices emerging from the data, we have inferred young people's basic questions, the fourth constituent of a world view.[6]

The popular arts help young people to ask and answer:

- How can I be happy?
- What prevents happiness?
- How can this be overcome?
- Who am I?
- To what group do I belong?

These inferred questions show partial overlap with the questions Wright considers central to world views in general, and a Christian world view in particular: 'Who are we? Where are we? What is wrong [with the world]? What is the solution?' Yet they differ in terms of scale. Young people's problems and solutions belong to a midi-, not a meta-, narrative. While young people want to know who they are as individuals and to what group they belong, a wider social identity, suggested in 'Who are *we*?' does not appear relevant. More energy is devoted to working out social identity on a smaller scale. 'Where are we?', a question in relation to a teleology, a cosmic end point, does not appear to arise, except in the sense of locating life experience in terms of either the actual or ideal world. Shifting back and forth between the Actual and the Ideal seems to provide a sufficient sense of movement. The only real threat is 'getting stuck' either through commercialism, or through a personal failure to 'get a life'.

A silent, 'depressed' dimension to the world view?

Since life is considered to be 'basically OK', and resources are thought to be available (through family, friends, popular arts), to fail is to be culpable. Sadness is not easily acknowledged in the face of 'achievable' happiness. For this reason, sadness may be a powerful source of hidden shame and loneliness for young people. If either the financial resources, or the security provided through family and friends are not available, our guess is that a 'depressed' dimension lurks beneath the Happy world view. If this is so, it is largely a silent dimension in so far as the young people did not talk about it with us or to one another during the interviews. There was little articulation of it beyond curt, dismissive utterances: 'sad', 'pathetic'. Indeed, we might speculate that apparent lack of space in this world view to discuss disappointments and failings might be a contributing factor to the rise in teenage suicides – when it is not acceptable to talk about such feelings, young people might act on them instead.

We have suggested that young people's happiness is to some degree dependent upon movement between the Actual and the Ideal. Psychological studies show that as the gap between a person's actual and ideal self widens, the risk of depression significantly increases. Subcultures (not sampled in our research) which do not, or cannot, subscribe to middle-class immersion in the popular arts, may present opposing world views. The nihilism of the Goth subculture might be one such mirror image. In our research, it was when young people interacted with images that they came closest to articulating life's irresolvable problems. Nevertheless, the problems articulated generally belonged to 'other people', not to the young people themselves (see Chapter 6).

Can this Happy world view be expected to survive into adulthood? It may be that this is a childlike world view that young people will eventually outgrow, but our guess is that young people are echoing broader cultural trends which the Church cannot afford to ignore.

Did we get this right?

Our aim through the semi-structured approach to interviewing was to let the young people raise their own concerns as far as possible. In other words, we wanted to see what was salient to them, rather than impose our own interests upon them. Did we get this right? Would we have found a different picture had we asked the young people more directly about their world view, and in particular the place of religion and spirituality within it? Related research suggests not.

The findings of our study are also confirmed by research carried out independently, but around the same time as our study (2002–2003), in the United States. This is the National Survey of Youth and Religion: 'a nationally representative [telephone] survey of 3,370 English and Spanish speaking teenagers between 13 and 17, and of their parents',[7] and 267 in-depth personal interviews with teenagers. The researchers for this National Survey found that: (a) mainstream religion 'mattered' to most of the teenagers they interviewed; (b) their religious beliefs and practices were highly conventional – and they were happy with that; and (c) while the teenagers' religious beliefs and practices were 'important' and conventional, they remained in the *background* of most teenagers' lives, and were rarely in the foreground of young people's world view.

Teenagers were more interested in other things such as sport, movies, music (i.e. popular culture), family, friends and romantic relationships. Moreover, despite the importance given to religion in the United States, the teenagers interviewed were quite inarticulate about their beliefs and had relatively little knowledge of the tradition they subscribed to – they were simply following in their parents' footsteps, and did not find anything to rebel against. Smith and Denton summarized the underlying religious framework that cut across faith and denominations as 'Moralistic Therapeutic Deism', which has the following implicit creed:

1.   A God exists who created and orders the world and watches over human life on earth.

2.   God wants people to be good, nice, and fair to each other, as taught in the Bible and by most world religions.

3.   The central goal of life is to be happy, to feel good about oneself.

4.   God does not need to be particularly involved in one's life except when God is needed to resolve a problem.

5.   Good people go to heaven when they die.[8]

The title 'Moralistic Therapeutic Deism' indicates the young people's view is that religion is 'good for you' in so far as it provides people with a moral framework, which they feel is essential for a good and happy life. Importantly, 'feeling good about oneself is an essential component in moral living'.[9] Following on from this, the second component of Moralistic Therapeutic Deism is that religion is found to be something that helps people to feel 'good, happy, secure [and] at peace'.[10] Finally, God's role in this is to help people feel better about life. God is called upon to intervene when needed, but otherwise is quite distant:

> The God of contemporary teenage Moralistic Therapeutic Deism is primarily a divine Creator and Lawgiver. He designed the universe and establishes moral law and order. But this God is not Trinitarian ... This God is not demanding. He actually can't be, because his job is to solve our problems and make people feel good. In short, God is something like a combination Divine Butler and Cosmic Therapist: he is always on call, takes care of any problems that arise, professionally helps his people to feel better about themselves, and does not become too personally involved in the process.[11]

An interesting point from our study and the research mentioned above is that in both the United States and England there appears to be an absence of young people being involved in explicit spiritual seeking, or claiming to be 'spiritual but not religious'. There is currently a great deal of discussion around the question of whether spirituality has taken over from religion (or is in the process of doing so). Popular culture is full of references to the supernatural realm, and this is sometimes taken as evidence that young people are bored with the Church but nevertheless engaged in some sort of spiritual quest. As we have argued above, we have not found this to be the case.

The spirituality we have uncovered is formative, based in the normal day-to-day relationships of everyday life. Popular culture is used as a vehicle to facilitate this process. There is very little transformative spirituality in the sense of young people searching out transcendence, and even when there is it tends to be within a (vague) framework of Christianity. Far from young people entertaining alternative spiritualities, Christianity is the default (if background) religion. Collins[12] found the same, and so did the National Survey of Youth Religion:

> Any teenage interest in practicing the spiritualities of other faiths or being 'spiritual but not religious' is present among only a very small minority of teens. Most, in fact, have not even heard of the spiritual but not religious mantra, and many of those who have do not really know what it means ... The vast majority of US teens are simply too conventional to consider, much less actively pursue, the idea of an eclectic spiritual quest. Again, however they were raised seems to be good enough for most.[13]

The subtle differences, as well as the overlap, between American and English youth are illustrated by Collins's research in England in 1997. For the majority of 13- to 15-year-olds she researched during the 1990s the realm of the transcendent was uncertain, dim and generally irrelevant to their everyday lives. In the main, faith was organized around family, friends and the reflexive self (Collins called this 'immanent faith'):[14]

> I love me and my family and friends. No other Gods. I believe in myself. (Young woman)[15]

> I believe in myself and my family. I am my God. (Young man)[16]

Religious symbols and references to a transcendent realm (mainly framed according to traditional Christian ideas) could be drawn upon in an emergency when the immanent faith structure was under threat. For example, young people might pray for a sick friend or dying relative, but on the whole the religious ideas did not play much of a part in young people's everyday lives at all. When the young people in Collins's study were asked directly what was most important in life they generally responded by saying it was to secure personal happiness through trusting relationships with family and close friends, and through various means of self-realization such as personal achievement and self-expression. In the short term, personal happiness generally meant 'having a laugh with friends' and passing GCSE exams. The young people's hope for the future then lay in one day having a family of their own (or at least a special, trusted and committed partnership with another), a job they enjoyed and a reasonably comfortable lifestyle. As with our current study, family was perceived to have an enduring significance across generations and to carry with it an obligation to love and accept each family member as they are. 'They are you, they're your flesh' (Young man).[17] Even if this was not lived out in practice, it was what young people felt should be normative. Therefore, failure to meet this expectation was felt keenly.

These findings correspond with Luckmann's suggested themes of the modern sacred cosmos: inner self, familism and forms of self-realization.[18] It also fits well with Robinson's work on non-churchgoers. On the basis of the British Values Survey, he argues that family, friends and leisure are of most importance to people and give meaning to life.[19]

This view is further confirmed by Heelas and Woodhead et al.'s recent work in England.[20] In a comprehensive study of the locality around the market town of Kendal in Cumbria, they explored the thesis that spirituality in the form of alternative religions, New Age and holistic practices, paganism, and so on (the holistic milieu) was taking over from conventional institutional religion (the congregational domain). They tried to compare like for like and so counted up the number of people involved in group practices of each type: those where the leader claimed the practices were 'spiritual', and those that had a building to meet in regularly. On this basis, they found that around 7.9 per cent of the population of Kendal attended church on a weekly basis, although this figure was in decline. This compared with just 1.6 per cent of the population who were actively involved in the holistic milieu. Furthermore, while alternative religions might be growing in popularity, the majority of people who participated in the holistic milieu were older, middle-aged women. The researchers found that just over 1 per cent of people who participated in the holistic milieu were between 20 and 30 years of age. They suggest this is the case because young people have:

> ... ample relationality by way of the mobile phone, the love affairs, the extensive friendship networks, the clubs and bars, the personalized work groups. Subjective-life is rich and full in such regards, which means there is little if any need for the holistic milieu to serve as a source of relational significance.[21]

It may be that in the future spirituality will take over from religion.[22] However, certainly for the time being, young people are happy to find meaning in their day-to-day world with family and friends, and engaging in popular culture.

Having (we hope) adequately established our argument, we now invite readers to immerse themselves in our young people's world view. Relish their creativity as they bend the popular arts to their own purposes, through TV soaps and film (Chapter 4), music and clubbing (Chapter 5) and culturally iconic images (Chapter 6).

PART TWO:
A CLOSER VIEW

The next three chapters immerse the reader into the world view young people enjoy through their use of the popular arts. They provide a greater level of empirical detail. Through this detail, we can clearly hear the 'voices' of our young people. Our different academic disciplines drew us each towards a particular popular art form – for example, we thought psychology, with its long history of studying visual perception, would be particularly 'good at' the analysis of young people's responses to culturally iconic images. So we each played on our own strength. Hence, Chapter 4, 'Story through soaps and films', is written primarily by Sylvia Collins-Mayo, a sociologist of religion. Chapter 5, 'Praxis through music and clubbing', is written primarily by Bob Mayo, a theologian and expert in youth work. Chapter 6, 'Symbol through image', is written primarily by Sara Savage, a psychologist. Each of us brought a particular perspective to the whole picture.

It was Bob who carried out most of the face-to-face group interviews (encountering primal events such as a fight breaking out, young people 'mooning' in the background, and mouthfuls of pizza dropped over our carefully selected images). These experiences, and a myriad of others (on the dance floor, in the youth clubs), enrich the theological reflections Bob provides in these three chapters.

If you feel that you are sufficiently familiar with the world of young people, and would rather simply consider the implications for youth work and the Church's ministry, you can move straight on to Part Three.

4

Story through soaps and films

A few months into our research, Bob led a residential week for young people who had little or no involvement with the Church and who were not particularly familiar with the Gospel stories. One evening he told the young people an updated version of the story of the prodigal son set in a modern context. Following the story there was a moment's silence, then one young man spoke up: 'That's me, that's my life.' The Gospel story had connected with his own personal story and to some degree had helped him make sense of his life and place in the world.[1] This is the power of stories, particularly those that are widely shared within a community or society, they give our lives meaning and locate the self in a comprehensible universe. It is through the telling of stories that we come to know who we are and what life is about.

Sadly, young people's knowledge of Christian stories is declining along with their general religious knowledge (see Chapter 2), but it is our contention that the popular arts have been useful in providing the symbolic tools for the creation of a shared story that enables young people to understand themselves and their world – the Happy midi-narrative. This chapter explores the role of films and British soap operas[2] in this process, looking in particular at Wright's four questions: 'Who are we?', 'Where are we?', 'What is the problem?' and 'What is the solution?'[3] We begin, however, with a reminder of our method and with an outline of some background features that inevitably affect the viewing experience of young audiences.

Method

To recap, we encouraged our young people, in the context of group interviews, to speak freely about their viewing habits in relation to soap operas and films. They were asked if they watched *EastEnders* and, if so, what storyline came to mind, and which characters appealed to them most. We also asked, 'What would you do if you were in that situation?'

Just as we encouraged the interviewees to speak freely about soaps, we also asked them to comment on their favourite films, or on films they had recently seen. For comparative purposes, we asked for comments about the following films: *Lord of the Rings: The Fellowship of the Ring*, *Harry Potter: The Philosopher's Stone*, *The Blair Witch Project*, *The Matrix*, *Star Wars* and *Terminator 2*. These films were chosen because the interviewees were likely to have seen them and because they suggested a connection with a meaningful reality beyond the material world.

Viewing experiences, choices and habits

We saw in Chapter 2 that young people are active and creative in their viewing habits. This has been aided by the widespread availability of various technologies – videocassette recorders, home filmmaking equipment, DVD technology, home computers, satellite interactive television, and so on, that have given young people direct access to the constructed nature of film and television programmes. Consequently young people are used to playing with these media and using the symbols they generate to create meanings relevant to their own lives.[4] During our group interviews we saw something of how the young people used soaps and films for this purpose.

Soap opera and film allow for two very different viewing experiences. Soaps offer melodramatic narratives focusing on the emotional ups and downs of personal relationships within families and communities (giving higher prominence to women than is usual in the film world). They have numerous ongoing storylines that interweave without marked endings, storylines designed to reflect the reality of everyday life. Indeed, the writers of *EastEnders* intended that the programme should have almost 'documentary reality'.[5] The impression of reality is enhanced by the fact that soaps are broadcast on the small screen and watched at home – a viewing environment which itself reflects, and even extends, the domestic character of soap life. Moreover, while the narrative has to keep going at a pace to retain viewers' interest, the impression of real time is created by the serial nature of the broadcasting. Viewers can tune into a soap world three or four times a week for an update, while characters' lives can be thought of as continuing outside of the viewing time. All of this contrasts markedly with the viewing experience offered by films.

Films cover a wide range of genres. Two films were spoken about most frequently, and thus were considered in most detail: *Lord of the Rings* and *Harry Potter*. These can both be loosely regarded as 'fantasy', with their emphasis on magic and mystery. Women in both of these films (and in most of the others mentioned during the course of the group interviews[6]), play secondary characters in the storyline. In contrast to soaps shown on television (and indeed films shown on television), the cinema setting in which these films are seen, takes the viewer away from the everyday world of home and family with all its attendant distractions and provides a neutral space in which new worlds can take shape.[7] In this respect, films, particularly fantasy films, offer expanded possibilities for the development of different worlds and realities in the minds of the viewers. In contrast with soaps, however, the narratives of mainstream films have a clear structure leading to a definite end, usually within a three-hour period. Even *Lord of the Rings*, which was presented as three separate, three-hour films over three years, had a conclusion. These basic differences between soap and film are important for our study, as genre and viewing context invite or inhibit the various types of interactions interviewees have with the media.

Soaps

Most of our young people were either regular or occasional viewers of *EastEnders*. They gave three main reasons for watching the soap. First, they found it entertaining. In particular, there was pleasure in escaping into another world and anticipating how the storyline would develop (see Appendix for a summary of the *EastEnders* storylines at the time of interviewing). They also enjoyed the humour in *EastEnders*. Secondly, there were social reasons: the young people enjoyed talking about the programme to their friends, gossiping and being 'in on the secret'.[8] Several of our young people also indicated they regularly watched soaps with other family members. Soap viewing crossed generations. Third was availability: *EastEnders* was a time-filler, a way of passing half an hour. During the research, *EastEnders* was being broadcast four nights a week at either 7.30 or 8.00 p.m., and repeated as an omnibus edition on Sunday afternoons. Most of the interviewees chose to watch the weekday episodes. The two-hour omnibus required a big time commitment and there was a suggestion that *EastEnders* still did not carry enough cultural capital to warrant such an investment in the way that a film might.[9] It was, however, fine for 'half an hour out on, like, Monday, Tuesday, Thursday and Friday' (Nicole).

The reasons other young people gave for not watching soaps reflected opposite viewing experiences to the positive statements put forward by fans: they were found to be boring, annoying or depressing, and watching soaps was seen as a waste of time – time that could be spent doing more pleasurable things.

> Amy: I prefer listening to music, speaking to someone on the phone – anything other than a soap opera. Go on a bike ride, doing exercise . . .

> Luke: I watch *EastEnders* when I am extremely bored and got nothing to do. And it's the same, like, when I am playing on [the] PlayStation. But when I do stuff like that I am, like, 'What am I doing? I am wasting my life!' And I get really, like, 'Ughhhh, go and do something else!'

Films

The reasons the interviewees gave for watching films were similar to those for watching soaps: they were attracted to an entertaining storyline that offered them an escape to an alternative reality, and rejected those that were 'boring' or 'mindless'. The young people went to films that had social cachet, either as the focus of a night out (usually with friends) or to provide a point of conversation later on. Films differed from soaps, however, in terms of their availability and were therefore watched in a more purposeful way. Some films were eagerly anticipated and watched at the earliest opportunity, and some, such as *Lord of the Rings*, inspired repeat viewings. Generally speaking, however, our young people did not 'drop in' on films and use them as time-fillers in quite the same way that they did with soaps, especially if viewing involved a trip to the cinema and some financial outlay. In this respect, films watched in the cinema required more effort on the part of our young people than soap viewing, but potentially this investment on their part was rewarded with a more exciting experience.

These three factors of entertainment, social relationships and availability kept the young people interested in the stories presented by soaps and films. In the following sections we turn to seeing how these popular arts contribute to young people's ability to make sense of their lives.

'Who are we?'

In Wright's framework, stories help people address the key question 'Who are we?' This question is about group identity, although our analysis focuses on the question at an individual level – 'Who am I?' – since this was the level at which most of the young people's responses were set. We can be confident, however, that individual identity informs group identity and vice versa.

Soaps and films provided our young people with a symbolic resource that could contribute to their negotiation of self in a wider context. This resource operated in a number of different ways, both inside and outside the text.

Ideal self

Perhaps the most obvious way in which soaps and films informed the interviewees' sense of self was through the presentation of alternative selves and the demonstration of different ways of being through the storyline and characters. This was part of their entertaining 'escapist' function. They opened up a space in which the current experience of self (which we call the 'actual' self) could be bracketed out for a bounded period of time and the imagination engaged to play with the possibilities of other selves, free from the restrictions of present reality. Films were particularly suited to this as they were able to bracket out the 'real world' to a greater extent than soaps – soaps having to maintain their realism by virtue of their genre. For instance, in film the viewer could draw on magic or superpowers in their escapism:

> Bob: So what is the appeal of *Harry Potter*?
>
> Ray: The little kids who want to believe in magic.
>
> Steph: I was trying to work it out why, because he [Harry Potter] comes from a very unprosperous background . . . Being special, and that is what everyone wants to be – everyone wants to be special.
>
> Ray: And everyone likes magic and mystery, so . . .
>
> Carol: And it is funny as well.

The young people's comments here suggest a process not too far removed from the imaginative play of early childhood. In other discussions, the interviewees identified characteristics and traits that they admired and would like to have themselves – and thereby began the process of imaging a 'special' ideal self. The main traits they identified in this respect were strength, authenticity and good looks.

Strength

Strength was interpreted as the ability to stand up for oneself, to be 'cool' and in control. This was identified in the soaps and films as physical prowess, special knowledge or sheer force of will. For example, the favoured characters in *EastEnders* were Kat Slater, Phil Mitchell and Steve Owen: Kat 'can stand up for herself' (Winnette), Phil presents as a 'tough nut' (Nigel) and Steve 'has everything up his sleeve' (Frasier). From the films:

> I wanted to be in the scene [in *Lord of the Rings*] where they have the big fight with the big troll thing ... because I wanted to be the Elvin guy cos he was just so cool. And it was like, just the way that they looked so cool when they just stood there and they knew these things were coming for them. (Luke)

Authenticity

Our young people admired people with confidence and the ability to be true to themselves, without pretence. Kat Slater was liked because she was 'outspoken and she is not scared to say what she thinks' (Joanna). 'What you see is what you get with Phil' (Derek).

It was interesting to note that the greatest respect was given to those characters that combined these qualities of the ideal self. Strength alone tended to make the character appear rude or aggressive, especially in women (e.g. Pauline Fowler), confirming old gender norms; authenticity without strength made the character appear weak and annoying (e.g. Mark Fowler, Ian Beale and Little Mo).

Good looks

Good looks enhanced a character's popularity, despite any failings she or he might have in the storyline (e.g. Jamie Mitchell and Zoe Slater).

The notion of an ideal self raises the issue of role models in soaps and films. On the whole, our young people did not identify role models spontaneously, although when asked, their responses revealed quite conservative gender patterns. Traditional male stereotypes went unquestioned. Strong, successful men of action remained dominant (e.g. Phil Mitchell and Steve Owen in *EastEnders*). The idea of a caring, sharing 'new man' was virtually absent. The closest approximation the interviewees talked about was Mark Fowler from *EastEnders*, who was seen as merely a wimp by both the young men and young women.

Characters identified as female role models (such as Kat Slater and Mel Owen in *EastEnders*)[10] also embodied fairly traditional characteristics, in so far as they were young and pretty. Less traditional was the emphasis the interviewees placed on them being strong, independent women who would not be 'walked on'. Little Mo, despite her loyalty to her (abusive) husband Trevor Morgan and her 'sweet nature', was regarded as too weak to be a role model. Only when she stood up to Trevor did she command the young people's respect. The older women were not identified as role models at all.

Actual self

Constructing an ideal self from the potential motifs in soaps and films required an imaginative projection of the actual self into new possibilities that are different from the here and now. Another process the interviewees engaged in, however, allowed a closer interrogation of their actual self: this was the more direct process of identification. Here the young people felt able to project their actual self onto a character or storyline, which then reflected the image back to themselves so that it could be used in the reflexive process of self-understanding. Soaps, because of their realism, seemed to be particularly useful for this type of exercise. Interestingly, when the interviewees identified with a character, it was partly because they saw them as either flawed or just unremarkable. In other words, actual selves were not the strong or glamorous types of the ideal self previously considered. Actual selves are more 'human'; they have problems and weaknesses as well as strengths:

> I like Zoe. I think she is me really . . . because she is very pretty and she knows she's young, you know; she has the same girlie problems as real girls. (Lyn)

> I like Ian, yeah. He's the kind of guy that some people can relate to. He has been really unlucky and I personally can relate to that. (Steve)

The young people seemed to find some comfort by comparing their lives to those of characters in a film or soap and seeing they were not alone in finding life difficult sometimes. It could even be a cathartic experience for our young people to see others worse off than themselves:

> I like to see someone worse off than my life; just to make sure that you are not actually right at the bottom. (Jeanette)

> I think it [music or film] shows you that, 'hey, you're not the only
> one going through something difficult; or hardship'. (Brian)

> You want to watch someone else's life being worse than yours
> and then you feel good about your life. (Steph)

There is, therefore, a sense in which soap and film helped the interviewees
locate themselves in a common humanity with all its ups and downs.

'Where are we?'

'Where are we?' is the second of Wright's existential questions. In the context
of our research, this question addresses the nature of actual and ideal worlds
as experienced by our young people. We could get a picture of the young
people's answer to this question through their comments about how true to
life soaps and films were. This was a natural judgement for them to make.
Indeed Ang found in her study of *Dallas* audiences, that the pleasure of
watching soaps was 'inextricably linked to questions of realism'.[11] Those who
found it realistic enjoyed it more than those who did not.

In order to make sense of her findings, Ang distinguishes between two levels
of realism: 'denotation', which concentrates on the extent to which the soap
content literally represents reality; and 'connotation', which is concerned with
whether or not the content resonates with the viewers' experiences on an
emotional level, so that it is at least recognizable, or *believable*, if not literally
real. Those people that found *Dallas* most realistic, and therefore most
entertaining, were those who focused on connotation rather than denotation.
For our young people too, a degree of connotative realism was important if a
film or soap was going to be enjoyable – the storyline and characters had to
be believable. This was particularly so for soaps, since the interviewees knew
the genre claimed to at least approximate reality. In this respect we found the
young people's comments on soaps tended to highlight properties of their
actual world, whereas their discussion on film allowed us a closer look at their
ideal world.

Actual world

The young people's opinions were fairly evenly divided on how realistic
EastEnders was. Those who took a more denotative approach found it
unrealistic in terms of the behaviour of individual characters and particular

storylines, but their main contention was that too many problems, difficulties and hardships were concentrated in such a small community and life is not actually like that.

For those who did like soaps, the redress to this complaint was that while the concentration of events was unreal, the events themselves were true to life and something with which people could identify. This identification with situation, if not for themselves then for others, was important. The young people suggested it gave the audience a valuable opportunity to think about issues and how they would deal with them in their own lives:

> I think a lot of people can probably identify with her [Little Mo], like what she is going through, so it is an important kind of plot. (Izzy)

Should reality be truly represented, they argued, it would not make interesting television – it would be far too mundane and boring.

> Derek: So much happens in just one street. I mean, a dead body under the patio; someone's house burns down the following week . . .
>
> Val: It's just too much.
>
> Errol: Yes, but they are not going to have people just doing boring stuff otherwise no one's going to watch it . . .
>
> Derek: I know, but they have got to keep it to a limit haven't they?

Taken together these views suggest that while young people recognize the real world has problems it is certainly not all bad. Indeed, for the most part, life is OK.

Moreover, when the interviewees were asked whether they, or anyone they knew, was in a situation similar to any of those experienced by *EastEnders* characters they generally answered 'no'. This gave a sense that although bad things happen, they mainly happen to 'other people'. And even if bad things do happen, the young people suggested that help would be available to them. Indeed, part of the function of soaps was to alert audiences to resources for help. It was seen as a betrayal of both support services and the audience to ignore or misrepresent help that was available:

> I don't like the way they make out she [Little Mo] hasn't got any options because they don't bring up the subject of, like, helplines

and shelters and things like that. I think that is quite bad because loads of people do go to them if they are in that situation and they are kind of, like, as if betraying it. She has not got no way out. (Izzy)

Ideal world

Given that the actual world was seen as fairly unremarkable, and for some possibly a bit dull, it is perhaps not surprising that much of the entertainment value of soaps and (especially) films lay in allowing young people to escape into exciting imaginary worlds. From the comments the young people gave us it was clear that this was more than a cognitive exercise. Escapism was an emotional experience. As Dyer argues, entertainment is about experiences that contrast real-world problems with the feelings of utopia (ideal worlds in our terminology). Entertainment 'presents head-on as it were, what utopia would feel like rather than how it would be organized'.[12] Feelings of the Ideal for our interviewees were dependent on three things: a good storyline, the quality of production and authenticity.

Storyline

From the young people's comments, it is clear that for them a good storyline contains elements of novelty, excitement, promise, action (the latter was particularly important for the young men), and the triumph of good over evil:

> Normal life, it's just you are there all the time, it's just mundane. But if you have got, like, fantasy stuff, it is just totally different, but keeps you interested. It's just a totally new thing and it's just amazing. (Amy)

> [*Lord of the Rings* is] great. It's like good and evil, and the elves, and it's just really pretty trees and it just takes everything that you like and puts it in, and it's so cool. (Julie)

A good storyline also creates *believable* worlds. Such were the storylines of *Lord of the Rings* and *Harry Potter*, that the interviewees were more than willing to suspend disbelief. Indeed, there was almost a nostalgic feel to some of the young people's comments about the ideal worlds they created:

> [*Lord of the Rings* is] like a golden age that didn't really exist, but you would like to think that it did. (Ben)

> [*Harry Potter*] It is nice to kind of feel that there should be something like that, you know, you can go to Hogwarts. Do you know what I mean? (Izzy)

There was a sense that these films connected with the lost worlds of childhood imagination, innocence and playfulness, and they possibly even hint at a wish for something that goes beyond everyday experiences. However, the comments also indicate that our young people did not regard other worlds as potential realities in their young adult lives – they are just pretend. Fantasy takes people back to when they were 'little kids and they want to burst out, but they can't because we've got to be sensible' (Tanya). *Lord of the Rings* is 'just magical, everything you wanted to believe when you were a kid and, like, [now the] atmosphere is shattered' (James).

The interviewees also valued storylines that challenged their concepts of the actual world, stories that were thought-provoking or funny. Comedy is important for ideal worlds not only because it creates happy feelings, but also precisely because it subverts the real world.

Production quality

Gledhill makes the point:

> if we want to know how fictions gain hold of our imaginations so that they effectively become a central part of our 'real' lives on a day-to-day basis we have to pay attention to these properties of aesthetic form and emotional effect.[13]

This was certainly true of our data; a good storyline was necessary for creating an ideal world, but it was not sufficient to create the feeling of utopia. For this, the quality of production was important, and the interviewees were capable and harsh critics. They laid a lot of emphasis on the quality of acting, and especially scenery and effects. These were magnified on the cinema's big screen and were the key elements that differentiated the capacity of films to create the feelings of an ideal world from that of soaps. Good special effects gave rise to feelings reminiscent of wonder, even awe:

Patrick: [*Lord of the Rings* is] amazing.

Amy: It's beautiful.

Patrick: It's so well put together.

Amy: Amazing . . . it just builds the whole of the world . . . this whole amazing story that is so intricate and stuff.

> And it's just so well-written and just this amazing fantasy story that just takes you off to a whole different place.

> I thought the special effects in [*Lord of the Rings*] were just so fantastic. (Yasmin)

Athenticity

Authenticity was also important. For soaps this meant the production had to try to approximate reality. For films such as *Lord of the Rings* or *Harry Potter*, authenticity was judged in terms of how well the film represented the book.

Because authenticity was important, 'hype' was a problem. Hype took away young people's sense of happiness and replaced it with feelings of exploitation. This, in turn, made it harder to escape into the ideal world, since such awareness made the interviewees less willing to suspend their disbelief. In this respect the young people were not cultural dummies; they were well able to exercise critical distance and were aware of their place as a viewing audience – where they fitted into the whole entertainment structure alongside actors, writers and the production team of any programme or film.

> I watch [*EastEnders*], but I think it's all to do with ratings, isn't it? All these storylines happen because Channel 3 want to put *Coronation Street* on at the same time as *EastEnders*, and they want to see who's going to win. (Beth)

Thus the downside of hype had to be balanced against the potential for pleasure the film offered.

Summary

What can we say then, about how young people use soap and film to understand their worlds? It appears that there is a sliding scale between the Actual and Ideal. Soap, a genre with an emphasis on realism, provides a mirror that enables the young people to reflect on the actual world around them – the people they know, the issues they face. Soaps generate good feelings too – some excitement and anticipation of a developing storyline, and a sense of relief that one is not alone with one's problems (that, indeed, others are worse off). In so far as they do this, they allow the young person to enter into an ideal world for a while. Soaps are more engaging in this respect if they are not taken too literally, connotation is more useful for generating feelings of utopia than denotation.

Films seem to take the process further. Depending on the genre, films can play at the boundaries of reality rather more than soaps and, as such, they can offer a greater sense of escape and, therefore, greater experiences of the Ideal. This is facilitated by the viewing context of the cinema itself – the dark theatre minimizes distractions and the images projected on the big screen engulf the viewer. Films also last longer than the standard half-hour of a soap episode, giving the audience more time to engage with a different world at any one time. However, a believable storyline, albeit believable in its own terms, remains important if a film is to provide utopian feelings – too real and it becomes boring or too close to home; too unreal and it becomes ridiculous or annoying. Equally important in the escape to the Ideal was the quality of production and, in particular, the use of special effects (clearly pertaining to films more than soaps).

What is the problem? What is the solution?

The third and fourth questions Wright suggests world views address are 'What is the problem?' and 'What is the solution?' For Dyer, entertainment's ability to generate utopian feelings lies in the extent to which it engenders feelings that contrast with five important problems found in modern society: scarcity and inequality; exhaustion from alienating work; dreariness and monotony; a sense of being manipulated; and feelings of fragmentation.[14] Analysts of soap and film have found this to be a useful framework of analysis.[15] The question we address here, however, is how did our interviewees interact with the problems represented in and by soaps and films?

The most obvious representations of real-world problems were found in soaps. Over the course of the research period, a number of different storylines were presented in *EastEnders*. Our interviewees mentioned 23, and of these 16 could be directly related to at least 10 problematic social issues: child abuse, paternal rights, infidelity, domestic violence, male rivalry and violence, mental illness, drug abuse, teenage pregnancy, bankruptcy, euthanasia and racism. It is our contention that these issues in the real world are united in the young people's minds as problems that prevent individual happiness, preventing access to the Ideal.

Films and soaps help young people identify issues in the actual world and facilitate the process of finding solutions to these problems, thereby forming a bridge between the Actual and Ideal. Young people do this through the subsequent discussion of storylines with friends. This helps the young people think through how they would cope in a situation similar to that represented. It provides an opportunity for contingent ('what if?') thinking:

Amy: I quite often get myself thinking about what I would do if I was put in that situation, even in a film like *Toy Story*, you can say, 'What would I do?'

Bob: Does anyone else do that, or is it . . .

Julie: Yes.

Luke: Yes.

Bob: You do think what you would do? Can you give me an example from a film where you thought, 'What would I do?'

Amy: Films with embarrassing moments. I think everyone thinks, 'Oh what are we going to do about that situation?'

Julie: Makes me think, like, what would I do if I was in a horrible accident? How would you begin to cope? And things like that.

Amy: . . . died of cancer and that kind of makes you think, like, what would I do in that situation and stuff? It makes me appreciate my mother.

Julie: I think films are able to do that to you and have some meaning.

Indeed, the interviewees enjoyed applauding or criticizing the behaviours of the characters according to whether or not they identified with their actions. Interestingly, however, most of this contingent thinking remained safely within the confines of the storyline. Rarely did the interviewees open up the discussion to talk about the issues in the wider context of the real world. To some extent this had the effect of keeping them distanced from the issues, as they remained something that happened to 'other people'. This may have been important in order to maintain the pleasure of escapism.

Two main solutions were given by our young people to the problem of hindered happiness: self-reliance and supportive family. These came through particularly clearly in the young people's responses to two main storylines in *EastEnders*: the abuse of Little Mo by her violent husband, Trevor; and the storyline concerned with the parental rights of 'hard man' Phil Mitchell over his daughter Louise.[16]

In the case of the Little Mo and Trevor storyline, very little attention was given by the young people to the issue of domestic violence per se, or to the perpetrator, Trevor. Rather, discussion revolved almost entirely around Little Mo's reaction to her plight. As far as the young people were concerned, Little Mo should have taken responsibility for her own happiness and stood up for herself against Trevor.

> Well, I didn't understand why she was such a doormat and how she keeps going back to him, do you know what I mean? (Sarah)

> If I had somebody doing that to me, I would just do something back. I couldn't just cower like she has been doing for years. I think when she left him and things, I think she was really good to do that because she at least showed him that she had courage. (Lyn)

The solution to the problem, therefore, was strong individuals working out their own salvation. This theme was picked up elsewhere. For example, one group talked about an older *EastEnders* storyline concerning euthanasia. In this case the issue did get contextualized outside of the storyline, but what remained clear was the young people's sense that people should take responsibility for their own happiness, even to the point of death:

Izzy: I thought it [euthanasia] is definitely something that needs to be brought up because there are all these laws and differences.

Sarah: In Holland it is legal, and plus there's that story with that woman with motor neuron disease, and she could kill herself so like . . .

Izzy: It does kind of give dignity. Why should [they stay alive], if they have   no reason . . . like, they can definitely not survive, they should be able to, like, be killed.

Bob: They should be allowed to, you think?

Izzy: Yes, definitely if it makes them happy, knowing that they can rest and stuff.

Sarah: Yeah. I mean I have seen, like . . . dying with cancer and it is not that pleasant . . .

Izzy: Yeah, your last moments should be happy.

Bob: So people should be allowed to die?

Sarah: Yeah, definitely.

Matt: Die, die!

Bob: Is that what you think as well?

Matt: I don't know.

Bob: Because sometimes people say it's not your position to say, like, you can kill people.

Matt: There is a point when I just think, well, you know, sort it out, you know, and just do it. Some people don't want to live at all, do they? And, you know, I think if they don't want to live at all then they should just be free to end themselves.

The above quote suggests that the young people's moral thinking in this area is not linked to transcendent values but rather to the imperative within the Happy midi-narrative, to be happy. We can also note, at this point, that our young people's comments about good and evil were always contextual. Hence they did not see goodness and evil as inherent realities in the world, but as a part of a storyline used to illustrate the real problem of individuals failing to make their lives better for themselves:

Bob: Do you like the element of good and evil [in *Lord of the Rings*], or is that nothing to do with it?

Andy: The badness, yeah? I mean I think it's always important to sort of project that in a film.

Phil: I think that about everything because it shows you that even right now, if we try to do anything, that you will have the obstacles – that life brings obstacles and you've just got to learn how to balance and don't let them get in the way [of where] you want to get.

The second main *EastEnders* storyline, around Phil and Lisa's baby, took the problem of finding personal happiness into a wider social context. For the interviewees it offered a moral dilemma: Lisa's personal happiness as a wife and mother against Phil's as a father. On the whole, the interviewees were clear that although Phil would not obviously make a good father – which did raise some misgivings over him knowing about Louise – he should nevertheless be told and should have access to her because it was his right as a father. Mark, as potential stepfather, had no right to stop him:

I felt when she [Lisa] didn't want him [Phil] to know, I thought she was wrong because if I had to hide it from someone, I

wouldn't want to because it's a baby, he has a right . . . to know.
(Lyn)

The key point here is that the kinship of blood ties was seen by our young people as being a highly significant part of the solution to unrealized happiness. To paraphrase the words of Big Mo in *EastEnders*, 'family is important because when the chips are down that's all you've got'. Family were seen as a key source of support when problems arose. Kinship breakdown is therefore highly problematic for young people because it deprives them of a source of unconditional support that has the potential to take them from the problems of the actual world to the happiness of the Ideal.

If kinship was regarded as part of the solution to life's problems, other relationships were not – at least not to the same degree. There was recognition of the complexity of personal relationships: marriage breakdowns, infidelity, and so on. In this respect, romantic relationships were seen to be as much a part of the problem as the solution. They had to be negotiated and worked upon, and trust in the relationship had to be established. While these relationships might be satisfying, they could not be taken for granted in the way that kinship could or should be. Thus, regarding the storyline about Jamie's infidelity to Sonia and his subsequent repentance and proposal of marriage to her, the interviewees were clear that Sonia should not rush into anything: she and Jamie had to work on the relationship together.

Formative spirituality through soaps and films

We started this chapter with the intention of exploring how the stories of soaps and films inform young people's world view. We have seen that there is a complex interaction between these media and the young people as audience, in which both the storyline and the viewing context are important. As the young people become engaged in the storylines, so they talk about them to their friends and adopt symbols useful for understanding their actual selves and their world, and for constructing a sense of the Ideal.

The narrative they refer to is consistent across the young people we interviewed. There were very few discernible differences according to demographic variables. In this narrative – the Happy midi-narrative – the actual world of young people appears to be fairly benign. Although bad things happen and people make mistakes, there is a sense that one can work to make life better, especially with the help of supportive family. The Ideal for which one works is an extension or intensification of the Actual. It is a world of happiness where the individual's potential is fully realized. The individual is authentic, strong and in control, and the ideal world is one of pleasure, excitement and action. Soaps and films are themselves part of the Actual and provide a bridge between the Actual and the Ideal. They supply the symbolic resources for young people to work out appropriate solutions to the problem of unrealized happiness in their daily lives; they offer a vehicle for contingent thinking and also an experience of the Ideal itself, as young people periodically escape into new worlds to forget about their actual lives for a while. In this respect, the interviewees have no need for a transcendent reality that locates the Ideal somewhere else. Even the idea of good and evil appeared to be reduced to little more than a formulaic storyline.

It is, however, important that soaps and films be believable, at least in their own viewing context, if they are to be effective in helping young people shape their world view. In this way they can provide a point of reference from which young people can explore ideas and issues. There is a parallel here with Wright's argument that Jesus' teaching operated within familiar (actual) settings, but subverted the taken-for-granted explanations of the first-century world view and opened up the possibility of entering the Ideal. In his case the Ideal *was* a transcendent reality. For our interviewees the Ideal is an intensification of the meaning and experience of happiness they already find in their everyday lives.

In sum, we have found soaps and films to be rich resources that young people can and do use to engage in *formative* spirituality. These media help young people to create meaning in their lives, and periodically provide experiences of raised awareness of relationality, moments of wonder and hints of mystery. We did not find, however, that this engagement led the young people to pursue further questions of a spiritual nature, to ask whether the Ideal they periodically glimpsed or imagined through these popular arts could be indicative of a reality beyond their world, rather than being firmly limited to the worlds created by imaginative writers and technologically sophisticated special effects. In other words, we did not find our young people engaged in transformative spirituality through soap operas and films. The world view of Generation Y in this respect remains largely secular.

Theological reflection on story

Story is a natural medium of expression for a young person finding her or his place in the world. Telling stories about things that have happened is the most straightforward way for a young person to work out what she think of herself, of others and of her experiences. Savage[17] picks up on this and describes a 'narrative' model of personhood. The 'narrative' model is one in which the young person develops into the person they are to become through their 'story' of their own life experience. These stories shape who people are and who they will become.

Savage refers to a 'container' model and a 'relational' model of self. The Church has traditionally held to an implicit 'container' model of self as earthly container, which houses the Spirit of God.[18] This understanding of self emerges out of the idea that people are empty vessels to be filled with the Holy Spirit and the truth of Christ. The young person's response to the truth of God, revealed in Jesus Christ, is then seen as determining the person they will become. Container-like metaphors do abound in Scripture, for example, 'we have this treasure in clay jars' (2 Corinthians 4.7). While the container metaphor is 'true' in so far as it is an appropriate metaphor for some aspects and functions of self, in practice it has come to mean in Christian circles that the inferior, bodily container is set against the superior 'filler'. This dichotomy borrows from some Greek philosophies, which denigrated the material, bodily aspect of the human person while elevating the spiritual and intellectual. To young people who consider their bodies and emotions as integral aspects of their being, this dichotomy is strange indeed.

Youth work, by contrast, tends to operate with a 'relational' model of self. This 'relational' model understands that the young person's development is dependent on close and significant relationships: these relationships help shape the person they will ultimately become. The role of the youth worker is, then, to spend time with the young people developing these relationships.

The research identified the huge importance young people give to relationships. Relationships provide a context in which young people's stories can be worked through. How these stories are told and how they are heard are significant in defining the young person's eventual sense of self. This means that it is not sufficient for Christian youth work to base itself entirely on a 'relational' model of youth work. Youth work needs also to operate according to a 'narrative' model. This would see the youth worker not only building relationships with young people, but also working with those young people in how they understand and tell stories of their experiences.

The research identified a lack of underpinning knowledge of the Christian faith. This means that when a young person tells a story about what they consider to be important, funny or significant, they are likely to be doing so without any reference to a wider framework of Christian belief. The challenge to the Church is, first, to listen to young people telling their stories, but then to make it possible for those young people to see their stories as a part of God's ongoing narrative of salvation. How can the stories people tell about themselves be developed from being simply self-expression and personal anecdotes, to becoming a part of a formative spirituality? And how can this formative spirituality become part of a transformative spirituality?

We can start this process by introducing stories from Scripture at an early stage in any relationship with a young person. Weston[19] writes about how there can be an assumption within the Church that Scripture needs to be introduced carefully so as not to annoy young people who have had a bad experience of the Church. The assumption is that any references to the Bible must come out of stories, relationships and shared experiences between the individual Christian and the young people. These experiences are then used to reflect back on to the Bible. However, we think that because young people often know very little about the Bible, youth workers can talk about it straight away. Scripture used in a non-prescriptive, non-judgemental manner is less likely, than has been the case in the past, to be met with hostility. Young people can draw from the Christian tradition, in the same way that they already draw from popular art and culture, to shape their identity. Scripture can be used to offer reflections and insights into the young person's experiences, and Christian awareness can come as a gradual process of discovery rather than in an instant moment of realization.

A Christian understanding of revelation goes beyond a formative self-awareness. The implication of God's revelation through Jesus Christ is that someone can only fully understand their place in the world through locating their own personal story within God's wider story of salvation. This moves the formative spirituality of story towards transformative spirituality. Transformative spirituality develops out of some form of 'appropriate and intentional participation in the redemptive activity of God'.[20] This redemptive activity is itself a story. The Bible is the account of the gradual and progressive revelation of God told through stories. In the Old Testament, the first glimpse is of God (a person) with persons: Adam and Eve in the Garden of Eden (Genesis 1.27). The second glimpse is of God as a nomadic tribal God with Abram (Genesis 12.2). The third glimpse is God as the national God of Israel (Deuteronomy 17.14). The fourth glimpse is of God as an international God who commands the Assyrians as well as the Israelites (Isaiah 10.5). The final glimpse is of God as a supernatural God who will write a new covenant on people's hearts (Jeremiah 31.31).

Wells[21] describes this narrative as a five-act drama: Creation (Act 1), Israel (Act 2), Jesus (Act 3), the Church (Act 4), the End (eschaton) (Act 5). The Church (Act 4) lies between the important events of Christ's victory (Act 3) and God's ultimate sovereignty (Act 5). The most significant events have either already happened or else are yet to come. The Christian finds her identity, and the young person can become her ideal self, by becoming a living character in God's ongoing story of revelation.

5

Praxis through music and clubbing

Music is a soundtrack to everyday life.[1] It is the 'amniotic fluid' in which young people's identity develops.[2] The ever-present nature of music, and its reign through clubbing, led us to consider music as dominant among young people's practices.

What people do, how they act and spend their resources, expresses their values and priorities. Thus, implicit world views are revealed through praxis, 'a-way-of-being-in-the-world'.[3] We can expect that the ways in which young people use music and clubbing will make sense in the light of how they understand themselves and the world.

In short, we found that the listening habits of our young people suggest a 'mirror' to the self. Music is generally chosen to reflect what young people are already feeling. It reflects rather than forms their attitudes. Music is a comforting backdrop rather than a demanding presence; it enhances the ebb and flow of young people's feelings.

Young people usually listen to music while doing something else. It provides a familiar, ever-present 'soundscape'.[4] They use music to mark their territory, to create a comfort zone. Music is the aspect of popular culture that offers a safe space in which young people can consider how to construct, and reconstruct, their identities. Music carries the rhythm of their everyday experience, but it has a more limited role in terms of conscious, conceptual meaning making. Feeling, rather than thinking, is the goal. The stamp of the Happy midi-narrative is thus glimpsed: young people are at the centre, supported by and in control of the music-listening moment.

Method

To explore the role music plays in young people's lives, we played five music tracks in the group interviews. Our selection, following the advice of two young DJs, reflected a range of styles that would be current for young people.[5] The interviewees listened to 60 seconds of each track and were asked in an open-ended manner for their thoughts and feelings towards each one in turn.

Music accompanying mood

Most often, music is seen as an accompaniment, following or accentuating, rather than creating a mood.

> [Music] in a sense doesn't put you in a mood; it's how you feel when you put on a CD. (Errol)

> I generally like music but it has to suit what I am doing. (Jason)

> You've got to be in the right mood. (Amanda)

> Music accentuates if you are feeling a bit low. (Roy)

The genres of music we used (dance, R&B, garage and house) were not seen as purveyors of propositional truths, but rather as 'soundscapes'. This music is a background presence, it is 'just there'. As such, it provides a resource that helps the young people to build up a sense of their own identity, because, as an echo to mood, it is primarily about themselves. One young man described music as a soundtrack to his social life. This background role does not mean music is incidental. Rather, it is crucial to young people because they can listen to it all the time.

> The radio is just a part of every day life – so I always switch on the radio in the morning as soon as I wake up. (Jasmin)

It's the context that matters

Music is listened to at the same time as doing something else, such as:

- driving
- working out in the gym

- reading
- cycling
- spending time in my bedroom
- working
- riding
- cleaning my car.

Music is valued mainly according to how well it relates to the interviewee's own context, rather than according to its aesthetic qualities.

> [In the gym] you need something with a beat . . . and energy. You need something to keep going. It doesn't have to be deep and meaningful. You just want rubbish. (Jill)

Music is used or discarded by the young people according to how well it connects with their situation. They adapt music to fit their moods, match their needs, or underpin their activities. This links with Hebdige's concept of 'historical specificity', in which a response to popular culture is seen as time-specific, representing a solution or a response to a specific set of circumstances.[6]

Not surprisingly, musical genres quickly come and go. Redefinitions of young people's social identity occur through their discrimination in regard to these genres. One young woman described garage as

> Twentieth century rather than twenty-first century. (Shirin)

That music could be used and then discarded so quickly speaks of young people's confidence to experiment and adapt. Music enables choice, creativity and the confidence to experiment. These unfold as key virtues in the Happy midi-narrative.

Music means more to the interviewees, or is enjoyed more, when the time, place or activity for listening is clearly identified by them. Garage, for example, is more like underground music – it is played after midnight when the lights are out.

> I would be up to listening to it all night; it doesn't matter to me. (Bill)

The context might also be a particular state of mind associated with a piece of music. Music had been there 'to support [his] emotions' in a time of relationship problems with his girlfriend (Richard).

Identity

When listening to music, it seems, our young people reflect both on their actual self and on the person they want to become. One feature of the Happy midi-narrative is the relative ease with which the ideal self can flow from the actual self, with no hard and fast distinction between 'who I am now' and 'who I want to be'. We found that music can provide a bridge between the two.

> It makes you think of . . . guys riding cars, open-top Cadillac down some avenue in California. (Chris)

> It reminds me of driving up to my mate's house in London as well. You are just playing that music in your car and just driving down the motorway when it is pitch black and you are on, like, full beam and it's good. I like it, yeah. (Alex)

Music provided a bridge between young people's actual and ideal self in three ways:

- through connecting with the interviewees' memory of past events in their lives;
- through enhancing their enjoyment of the present;
- through offering them a way of interpreting dilemmas and choices in their lives.

Memory

It is often the memory the music evokes that is important, more than the music itself. As one young person said, the actual music could be incidental. Events that might otherwise have been forgotten are brought back into people's consciousness in connection to a particular track. Evidently, it is the track of music, as much as the actual event, which is being remembered. A circular enhancement occurs: a piece of music is identified with a past event, hearing the music triggers the memory, and in time enhances and idealizes the recollection of what has happened.

> Liz: [The music triggers] memories from being back home on a Sunday night . . . go, like, from pub to pub.
>
> Bob: That is interesting. So you like the music because it connects with memories.

> Liz: Yes.
>
> Bob: How do you respond to it, Zach?
>
> Zach: I liked it. I mean, good beat and rhythm and, similarly for me, memories of clubbing in Manchester.

This helps to provide a bridge between the actual and ideal self. The music connects with the actual self because it brings to mind events that might otherwise have been forgotten. It links with the ideal self because over time the memory recedes, but the music remains and becomes a part of a generalized and enhanced sense of self-awareness.

> Winnette: Yeah that's what it reminds you of . . . smoking the weed and . . .
>
> Bob: So you like it because it reminds you of a good experience, yeah.

Music as enjoyment

The most fundamental reason for the young people to listen to music is that music is relaxing and fun. Music signals the opportunity for a good time.

> [It] makes you want to move; makes you happy. (Patsy)

Enjoyment of music is described more in terms of the beat, rather than the lyrics of the song:

> If I was sat, like, in a mate's car . . . the bass cranked right up . . . the lyrics don't matter, not in that situation. (Ian)

While lyrics that speak about the actual world can be valuable and meaningful to young people, experiencing a degree of happiness (through enjoying the music or clubbing experience) appears to be paramount. By providing relaxation, fun and entertainment, music enables interviewees to feel happy with themselves and with their situation. The familiar backdrop of sound enables the young people to colonize the space they are occupying. The interviewees' (sometimes exasperated) arguments that music does not *need* to be anything other than enjoyable is in accordance with the logic of the Happy midi-narrative.

Meaning in music

Meaning in music, although not required, is nevertheless valued if present. Music is considered rich in meaning if it connects with the choices or dilemmas that the interviewees might have to face.

> When you are not able to say something, but through music you are able to express yourself. (Guy)

When music provides a mirror to the Actual, the Actual becomes a *transition point* to the Ideal. For the lyrics to be meaningful, they need to represent what life is seen to be like. One young person, for example, talked of hating music that is not connected to reality on any kind of level (Jill). Interviewees are not looking to music for a higher wisdom or insight, but for something that echoes what they have already worked out (or are in the process of working out) for themselves.

The groups that identified themselves as Christians made more connections between music and meaning, but there was no attempt to link meaning with religiosity. Meaning comes when the music mirrors actual experiences, hopes or ideas the interviewees recognize from their day-to-day lives. They did not indicate that they were seeking meaning by connecting their day-to-day living with a transcendent reality. Any significance is spoken about in terms of how *life is*, not in terms of a deeper underlying purpose.

By way of contrast, Beaudoin described popular culture as surrogate religion, an essential resource for people to make sense of life and to pursue personally authentic meaning. He speaks of popular culture as made up of texts that express particular views about the meaning of life in the same way as religious texts might do.[7] Lynch argues that the idea of a fixed meaning supplied by popular culture in a top-down manner is naive, and that their own interests and commitments shape people's understanding of popular culture.[8]

Our research findings concur with Lynch's conclusions. Our data indicates that young people were using music for their own purposes. They were not simply consuming pre-packaged meaning. The difference between Lynch's work and our research is that Lynch focused on an older group of people (Generation X, the generation before our interviewees). His work refers to the 'felt need' of Generation X-ers to find personal authenticity and meaning while not accepting pre-packaged parcels of meaning and truth. The young people in our research, however, were not driven to look for meaning and significance outside of their immediate context. They appeared free of the inherent dissatisfaction and quest often associated with Generation X-ers. Instead, it seems that they saw meaning and purpose as already intertwined within their own lives.

Music as significant

There were three categories of interviewees' responses showing music to be both enjoyable and personally meaningful. Music is of most significance to young people when enjoyment and personal meaning combine.

In the first category, when interviewees participate in making music, they discover the music to be significant:

> You put a lot more into a piece of music than just the words because there's a whole expression of music, the structure, the beat, the melody, everything you put into that is designed to convey your message. (Adrian)

In the second category, when interviewees strongly identify with the artist, they find more significance in the music. Soul music is important because it has a story to it. Women consciously identify with female singers: 'I guess they are more like you' (Lyn). Kylie Minogue appeals to both men and women because she is 'a cutie ... she has got this sweetness about her ... Women want to be her and men want her' (Helen). Mary J. Blige, on the other hand, connects because she has come through a horrible episode with drugs and alcohol, and now her latest songs are happier. Her story could be interpreted through the main storyline of the Happy midi-narrative: she aimed for happiness (through music), stumbled over obstacles (drugs and alcohol), but the problems were resolved and happiness was eventually restored. Interviewees appreciated the opportunity to listen to music that has emerged from the artist's own experiences.

The third category of significance arises when listening to music develops into conscious lifestyle choices, as in clubbing, punk rock or garage culture. Music provides an opportunity for the young people to define a social identity for themselves. Punk, for example, provided a medium for one person to express what she saw as her actual self. It was her way of acting out what she understood about the world.

> [Punk is good] because, I mean, for me it is ... language and protesting, and says something ... to me, about my life and

about the way me and a lot of my friends are feeling that the world is crap ... I don't know, just trapped in sort of external chaos and external oppression and internal chaos and internal oppression from living in a completely commercial world. (Jill)

Listening to a Walkman, iPod or MP3 player can become a part of identity formation, in that the music becomes a tool, helping the listener to assert a sense of control over space. It is a way of marking territory:

I hate them [my neighbours] so I put the music up really loud ... but most of the time I've got my Walkman on me. (William)

Music helps young people to make the context they are in comfortable or familiar, colonizing the space. The listening patterns of the young people help to define a social as well as an individual identity. Musical tastes are a part of delineating who is inside a particular social group (and who is outside). According to Bennett's notion of locality, responses to music emphasize distinctions between young audiences (and hence social identities).[9] This idea was supported in our data.

Bob: Is music a personal thing or is it something you listen to with other people?

Derek: It's a question of identity.

Errol: Yes, I think it's both ... If you take, like, the punk scene or something like that, it's not just the music that they love, it's the whole kind of package that comes with it.

Beth: [It is] clothing [as well].

Songs sung collectively in schools, for example, and among friends create a sense of unity in the same way the television programme *Pop Idol* provided a sense of social cohesion: 'The whole nation was gripped by it' (Jasmin).

One interviewee, as if she were making a confession, admitted to liking classical music. She said that listening to certain pieces of music could make the hairs on her arm stand up, but she assumed that people would find her weird because of it (Jill).

To recap, music is used mostly as a supportive, background soundtrack that is important to the interviewees in so far as it connects with their own personal context. Frith comments that music plays a central part in the construction of identities.[10] In our data, it was the young people, rather than music itself, inhabiting centre stage. In this way, the interviewees retain the position of central actors in their own soundtracked drama.

Commercialism

Our young people showed themselves to be fervent believers in the power of the consumer. The practices surrounding music and clubbing engender in them an exaggerated sense of agency. By judging a piece of music to be 'commercial' and refusing to buy it or to dance to it, our interviewees retain some sense of independence (however illusory) from the forces of commercialism. This sense of agency promotes a feeling (if not the reality) of movement towards the Ideal. They react against having their listening and clubbing experience pre-packaged, branded and commodified. Music that is too commercial is seen as 'cheap'.

> When music is made solely for making money . . . it just loses its point or its message or its potency, and really it's just nothing to enjoy. (Adrian)

While commercialism is seen as the 'enemy within' for both music production and clubbing, interviewees considered themselves as the ultimate arbiters concerning what is 'edge' in a constantly moving world. There is an inherent paradox in the relationship between the music chosen by the young people and the commercially driven music market. The paradox of commercialism works like this: music seen as 'edge' becomes popular and hence commercially successful. However, as soon as the music becomes commercially successful it loses the edge that made it popular in the first place.

> You won't get as much money underground, but when you get commercial you get more money. But then people just think the music isn't as good anymore. (Frankie)

Thus commercialism both enables and undermines the virtues of the Happy midi-narrative. It enables the Happy midi-narrative by providing a semblance of choice, while at the same time it undermines the Happy midi-narrative virtues of autonomy, spontaneity and creativity. Similarly, commercially driven dance centres create more options (a virtue in the Happy midi-narrative), but commercialism also means less creativity.

Commercialism is a default position against which the young people are constantly reacting. They see themselves as discriminating aesthetes; they are not passively absorbing what wider commercial interests serve up to them. Songs described as 'fat' are great; songs that are 'rinsed' have been played too often (a sure sign of commercialism). Music that gets stuck in your head is simply annoying. When music fails to be enjoyable or entertaining, young people's responses are merciless. The extent to which commercialism *grates* is illustrated in the sheer variety of comments made about music seen as commercially infected. The comments range from the apathetic to the apoplectic:

- would buy it . . . would get it off the Internet (Jenny);
- would dance to it (Steph);
- if they were playing it in a club I would not object (Ben);
- wouldn't switch channels but wouldn't buy (Shirin);
- wouldn't turn it off (Lucy);
- would sit down and probably come over all bored (Thomas);
- would walk out on it/leave the room (James);
- would throw it in the bin (Lucy);
- would throw my car radio out of the window (Abby);
- can't stand it. It makes me want to tear my hair out (Julie);
- revolts me to the pit of my stomach (Jill);
- get the DJ and smack him with the record (Thomas).

The number and type of negative comments made by the interviewees about the music are far more extensive than any parallel positive comments. These negative comments indicate a level of sophistication in being able to recognize when primarily commercial interests drive a song. It is also indicative of the nature of young people's intense relationship with the music as judge and jury. A certain glee was evident as they 'rubbished' particular tracks. Descriptions included:

- boring
- crap
- irritating
- trash
- repetitive
- rubbish
- sterile and false
- manufactured
- monotonous

- just a noise like all these Ecstasy tablets people are taking (Jack)
- The school report would say try harder . . . bottles of coke you expect to be fizzy and it's not – it's flat! (Jill and Alice)
- no musicality
- no talent.

Accessibility

Negative comments about music did not concern its accessibility or repeatability. They liked the fact that at times they felt that they could do just as well themselves. With a background beat, anyone could take the microphone and become a master of ceremonies (MCing) and then talk about 'whatever'. The music is democratized rather than elitist – music is something made and used, rather than something (reverently) listened to. Interviewees see themselves not just as listeners but also as participators in, and creators of, music. This attitude carries over to clubbing. Malbon describes how the individual creates rather than simply participates in the clubbing experience (if there are no clubbers then there is no club).[11]

The accessibility of music from the Internet is another feature in the democratization of music. Interviewees said that when they hear a song on the radio they like, there is no need for the inconvenience of having to wait to hear it again, or even of having to purchase it – instead they can download it, listen to it as and when they want, and then discard it in favour of the next song. One young woman had 17 different versions of 'Video Killed the Radio Star'.

> In earlier eras, it was the uniqueness of the painting or work of art, or the unrepeatable quality of a particular performance of music, which underwrote its claim to be an authentic work of art. In the world of the Walkman, the CD and the portable digital music player, it is the infinite repeatability of music together with its variability that is most striking.[12]

Clubbing

Malbon estimated that £2 billion was spent by British clubbers on their nights out in 1996, and 500,000 people went clubbing each week.[13] This was more than all spectator sports, theatre, live music, comedy and cinema combined. In

Malbon's seminal ethnographic study, clubbing is a vital context for the development of personal and social identities. As discussed earlier in the chapter, the importance given to music increases in proportion to the active participation of the listener: clubbing is a complete immersion. It is a collective activity, underscored by music, which produces a sense of social cohesion, exhilaration and unity.

Method

During our group interviews we asked: 'What is the best thing about clubbing?' 'What is the worst thing about clubbing?' 'Have you ever experienced anything out of the ordinary while clubbing?' 'Do you carry over anything of what you experience in clubbing to your everyday life?' We also carried out fieldwork in two London clubs.

In our group interviews, young people's widespread clubbing experience was framed implicitly within the Happy midi-narrative.

> The whole thing boils down to having a good time. (Daniel)

People go clubbing because it is fun, not simply as an escape from the oppression of work. Uplifting music in clubs left interviewees with 'a sense of euphoria' (Frasier). They see it as an opportunity to 'get rid of built up energy' and to 'be themselves' (Lawrence).

> The idea [of a rave is] to get away from this sort of, 'Oh it's got to mean something and it's got to be talented.' If it just, like, sounded good and made you dance, then that was it. (Derek)

Clubbing and religious experience

We wondered whether clubbing, as an intense, euphoric, out-of-the-ordinary experience, might be interpreted within a framework of religious experience. Despite our probing, we did not find the kind of transformative spirituality we were looking for. The best clubbing experiences were spoken of simply as a collective experience of unity and exhilaration.

> When the vibe is good at a club you can tell that everyone is on the same wavelength. You just look at people and you know it is going to be a good night. (Clubber)

> The last thing you think about is getting up for work the next morning ... [you] don't care about anything. It's sort of like building – you're just building your own community outside of, like, normal structures. (James)

> In an ideal clubbing world nothing bad happens – you can be yourself, as long as you allow others to be themselves (Lawrence).

The experience of clubbing provided the interviewees with an instant and emotional community, whose unity was created by a shared love of the music being played.

The best things for the clubbers we spoke to in London clubs were:

- getting together with your mates and dancing;
- being in an atmosphere where everyone understands what you are feeling;
- a feeling of total exhilaration;
- fried shoes;
- a million friends in one room.

Young people in the group interviews said:

- You can dance – just keep on going and just never feel you need to stop. (Stewart)
- The adrenaline and the music that it generates. It kind of lifts you up. (Chris)
- The moment out of your whole dull, sad, pathetic little life where I would, you know, feel in touch, and connected with something and not feel completely alone. (Alice)
- ... take me away from my reality. (Robin)

Clubbing can trigger a sense of freedom or euphoria, an oceanic experience.[14] The through-the-night timescale disrupts normal biological rhythms and brain function. Dance music, which has 'everything stripped away but the beat', has a 'mellowing' impact that lasts through the next day. There is a clubbing 'liturgy', which follows a pattern of extreme physical experience. The night out, shaped by music, generally climaxes midway between the pubs closing and the denouement in the early hours of the morning. The aim is to attain a stable peak time of 'high' when people are 'pissed', 'going higher' and 'enjoying'. After the high, people need help from the DJ to 'come down' through the right type of slow music, to pair bond or to simply 'chill out'.

The emphasis on simply having a good time indicated by our interviewees contrasts with some sociological literature which suggests that clubbing is indicative of a 'spirituality' or 'religiosity'. Olaveson highlights the experience of connectedness, often interpreted by ravers as a religious experience. He draws on the idea of collective effervescence in that a rave is inherently communal, infused by electricity ('the vibe'), ecstasy and enthusiasm.[15] For Heelas, there is evidence of a de-traditionalized present – people having what they take to be spiritual experiences outside a framework of institutional religious belief.[16]

In contrast, we found that while clubbing does provide an extreme communal experience, it is an end in itself. Our interviewees were realistic about the unity experienced through clubbing – those intense relationships rarely survive into the next week. The energy, hope and optimism engendered by clubbing evaporates at the end of the night and does not spill over to transform ordinary life.

We found that clubbing is rarely associated with spirituality or religion. On the rare occasions when it is, this is in an indirect, analogous way. The clearest connection made between clubbing and religion came, not in the group interviews, but in response to a question we posted about clubbing and religious experience on a clubbing web site (www.clubbing.com).

> I don't think people fully realize how important clubbing and the general clubbing scene is to us. It's a religion. Religion goes much further than beliefs. Religion is an escape. It's something people cling to. Without religion a lot of people would be lost in life. I personally have huge respect for the Catholic religion even though I am not really a believer. For example my parents would be lost if they had not the Catholic religion to cling to. When times are hard they always look to their religion and always seem to find solace in it. I think for us younger people who don't find much interest in the Catholic religion we find something [else] that we can cling to. For most of us clubbing is what we cling to. Pressures build up in all our lives but at the end of the week we find clubbing our escape route. Personally I'd go mad if I didn't make it to a club just once a week. I look forward to it. It kind of keeps me going in those dark depressing early days of the week. It's a chance to come into contact with other clubbers who hold the scene and music in such high regard. The centerpiece of our religion is the music. Something we can all worship and appreciate. We are all fanatical about our religion

and boards (websites) like this are proof of that. When we are away from our clubbing scene we all still want to keep the memory alive throughout the week. We come on this message board to be with people of our faith. We play music throughout the week and show unmatched devotion to it. Spirituality may not be the exact word I'd use but without doubt it's a religion that we clubbers need and have to cling and turn to at the end of the day. A more social form of a religion maybe but just as important to us.

That's my lot. Bullshit it may be but I do think there is some truth in it.

Yet even in this web site response, 'religion' is not defined as a connection with a transcendent reality (such as God), but as something social, cathartic and exuberant. It is what they take into the experience as an interpretative framework that defines the clubbing experience:

[Your clubbing experience] depends on the emotions and preconceptions in your brain. (Jill)

Role of the DJ

Clubbers are not passive absorbers of the music; they actively engage with it, or react against it. This shift from passive listener to active consumer mirrors the shift in the role of the DJ from passive player of records to virtual musician.[17] It mirrors the musical genres of sampling, MCing and mixing, styles reflected in the tracks used in this research (dance, house, garage, R&B).

From our interview and fieldwork data, it is clear that the club DJ (usually male) performs a pastoral role, an observation also made by other researchers. Saunders, Saunders and Pauli wrote about DJs as the high priests of the rave ceremony, responding to the mood of the crowd, with their mixing decks symbolizing the altar (the only direction in which ravers consistently face).[18]

The priestly metaphor, we suggest, is an example of a Christian framework applied to the role of the DJ. It is not language clubbers themselves use. However, a pastoral role is involved, and this was found in young people's talk:

You go to a club 'to lose your baggage'. (Lawrence)

He is the most important person. (Andy)

The DJ responds to the clubbers gathered, intuiting and enhancing their mood and taking them on a journey. The DJ selects and creates music, voicing the feelings of the crowd. He or she performs a cathartic role, and helps people to express, through dance, their 'agro' and frustrations.

> It's the job of the DJ ... You can sit there ... and we often talk about how do we approach this? Do we keep giving them up-tempo, you know? Do we keep them literally screaming at us? Or do we think, right, there is 45 minutes [to] an hour left – do we take them down gradually and leave them saying, 'Yeah, that was a good night,' or do we leave them at the end going 'We want one more record, we want another record'? (Lawrence, a DJ)

Even here, though, with all the power and responsibility for the evening invested in the DJ by the clubbers, the music still needs to resonate with what people are feeling. As 'pastoral workers', the DJs can only work with what the people give them. Clubbing requires a reciprocal commitment. In the vulnerable hours after 1.00 a.m., when fights can break out and people are feeling tired and hungry, the DJ offers 'options': music to enable people to pair up, or music to 'come down'.

Yet the most basic constraint is that the DJ has to follow the mood of people on the dance floor, selecting the music to suit what people are doing or feeling. If a DJ chooses an inappropriate track – makes a mistake – people are not going to follow that lead but will walk off the dance floor. The DJ is not the ultimate arbiter in the choice of music. The DJ cannot experiment if the crowd has not got a minimum level of musical knowledge and understanding to allow him or her to do so.

At the time of writing, clubbing, that once dominant praxis, has waned. By 2004, the British Phonographic Industry decided that the Brit Awards was to axe its 'gong' for Best Dance Act and replace it with a new live category. This followed the collapse in 2003 of three dance music magazines (*Muzik*, *Ministry* and *Jockey Slut*). Petridis wrote that it sounded like the final nail being banged into the coffin of what was once the most exciting musical genre-cum-youth movement in the world.[19] Part of the problem, he wrote, was that the clubbing scene was bound up with drugs, and that meant it had a short shelf life. Clubbing had lost its all-important cachet of cool.

Theological reflection

Affirmation and challenge are two separate strands that run right through Scripture. The idea of affirmation is exemplified in Jesus' statement that he has come so that people may have life and have it abundantly (John 10.10). The idea of challenge is illustrated by Jesus saying that if any want to follow him they must deny themselves and take up their cross (Luke 9.23). The experience of being either affirmed or else challenged by the Christian message is itself a foretaste of what the Bible describes as the ultimate realities of salvation and judgement.

Clubbing has its own versions of both affirmation and challenge. Affirmation comes through the intoxicating sense of pleasure for pleasure's sake. People go clubbing because it is fun. Clubbing is 'essential' – at least for a time: 'You have to do it'; 'You are only young once' (London clubbers). Play and fun can be overlooked as ways of understanding how people see themselves. However, for a young person learning to relate to the world these will be natural parts of experimentation and self-expression. Both of these are evident in abundance through clubbing. Malbon talks of this as playful vitality: 'a celebration of the energy and euphoria that can be generated through being together, playing together and experiencing others together'.[20] McRobbie wrote that current dance music pursues a logic of pure pleasure: it is enjoyment for enjoyment's sake.[21]

However, things can go badly wrong on a night out. As real as the excitement endemic to the temporary world of the clubber's own construction, is the possibility of judgement and challenge entering the clubbing experience on a lousy night out. It was regularly reported that the worst thing about clubbing was feeling wasted at 6.00 a.m. trying to find a taxi to get home. There were references to sex in toilets. There were different stories of violence associated with regular clubbing. Interviewees reported:

- getting sliced (Samantha);
- [getting] bottled (Jack);
- cigarettes stabbed out on your hands . . . many times (Shirin);
- one person raped . . . on the dance floor (Phil).

In the clubbing world the immediate, temporal reality is everything. It is the ethos of the carnival where the present moment is all-consuming. However, this collapses any idea of there being a clubbing 'salvation', because there is nothing transformational in a regularly repeated diet of fun and enjoyment. A night's clubbing is a self-contained experience. It is fun rather than meaningful. It is a euphoria that evaporates.

The impression of a clubbing 'salvation' is false because there is no transforming bridge of grace when things go wrong. Without a concept of grace and of being freely accepted by God, there is no possibility of crossing from judgement to salvation. If things go wrong, they go wrong, and there is no redemption on offer within that experience. The idea that, like Neo in *The Matrix*, 'you are the one', your very self is the doorway to the infinite and the eternal, is an illusion in regular clubbing experience. The reality of clubbing is that it can often be a crude and unsavoury experience; it often descends to the level of 'meat market', or 'cattle market':

> Eighty per cent of people go to clubs to meet a woman; 80 per cent of women go to clubs to meet a bloke. (Lawrence)

The overarching expectation is that clubbing involves 'getting drunk, having a good time and letting go', with the added possibility that 'if I pull, that will be a bonus'. Clubbing offers the illusion of an ideal based on the adrenaline, excitement and fun of an immediate and extreme experience. The high does not last. As one clubber lamented,

> You suddenly think, 'What the hell am I doing?' [And that is] when you hit 17. (Jill)

6

Symbol through cultural icons and advertising images

Symbols embody deeply held meanings and values. A flag can represent a whole nation; a wreath of poppies, valour, sacrifice, or a lost generation. Symbols draw us in; they impact our psyches at a level deeper than words. They do not function in isolation. In Wright's[1] terms, the symbol of the cross links with the story of redemption and the praxis of the Eucharist. Together, symbol, story and praxis create and make visible a world view.

In this chapter, we focus on the role of symbol in young people's world view – through images of cultural icons and advertisements. Symbols have the job of pointing out social boundaries. In fact, those who understand the significance of a symbol are a culture's 'insiders'. Those who do not are 'outsiders' by virtue of their ignorance: 'What on earth am I supposed to do with this little round wafer/wreath of poppies/secret handshake?'

It is this particular role of symbols as definers of boundaries that emerged most clearly through our group interviews with young people. Symbols tell us what is inside and what is outside a world view.

Method

Open-ended questions

We presented the young people with 15 cultural icons and advertising images during the group interviews. We piloted a range of images in advance, and our final images were selected for their potential to get young people talking, and to tap into underlying questions such as 'Who am I?', 'What is wrong?', 'What is the answer?'

List of images:

1. **Madonna** (cultural icon). Photograph of pop star Madonna, scantily clad, in provocative pose.

2. **Female runner** (cultural icon). Photograph of female athlete at the moment of crossing the finishing line.

3. **Male model** (cultural icon). Photograph of 'Hollywood-handsome' man, head and shoulders only, in thoughtful pose.

4. **Pregnant man** (advert). Health Education Council's contraception advertisement from 1970s, featuring a pregnant man with a huge belly.

5. **Newborn** (advert). Advertisement for Benetton featuring a newborn baby, bloody and wailing.

6. **Old and young** (cultural icon). A close-up black and white photograph of an elderly woman and young woman facing each other.

7. **Man dying of AIDS** (advert). Another Benetton advertisement, this one featuring a photograph of a man airbrushed to look like Jesus, dying of AIDS, with family in grief surrounding his bed.

8. **Prince Charles kissing Princess Diana** (cultural icon). Photograph of Prince Charles and Princess Diana kissing on their wedding day.

9. **David Bailey's anti–fur image** (advert). Anti-fur advertisement using David Bailey's photograph of a supermodel dragging a fur coat across the floor leaving a trail of blood. The slogan reads, 'It takes 40 dumb animals to make a coat but only one to wear it.'

10. **Munch's painting** *The Scream* (cultural icon). An Expressionist painting of a figure screaming against a background of a threatening sky.

11. **A soldier in the Gulf War** (cultural icon). Photograph of burning oil fields, solitary soldier watching in foreground, back to the camera.

12. **The Twin Towers** during the September 11th attack (cultural icon). Two photographs showing the Twin Towers of the World Trade Center during the September 11th attack: one of the second plane approaching the tower; one of the explosion following the second collision.

13. **Ali G on a cross** (cultural icon). Photograph of comedian Ali G on a cross.

14. **Buffy the Vampire Slayer** holding a stake (cultural icon).

15. **Deer in a forest fire** (this was a wild card thrown in to see what reaction it provoked). Photograph showing deer in a clearing, with a forest fire blazing all around.

We asked for our interviewees' thoughts and feelings in response to each image. Adolescents' reasoning, after the age of twelve, normally progresses beyond being tied to concrete, tangible realities, to the ability to use abstract, formal logic. This cognitive leap forwards among adolescents opens the door to philosophical, existential and religious questioning. And so we were interested in any signs of such questioning.

Task questions

We asked the young people to select one image to which they particularly related, and to explain their choice. Additionally, two group interviews were given an exercise in which the interviewees were asked to choose three or four images and group them around a story of their own making. What was important to us was the kind of thinking and interacting that occurred in response to images.

Visual perception has been intensively studied in cognitive psychology for decades. The data from our group interviews allowed us to compare responses to the task questions (in which the young people actively made their own choices, and/or told their own stories) to responses to open-ended questions. We also looked at differences between the groups' responses in terms of their gender, race, age, religion, location, size of group, and employment status.

Categories

Young people's conversation about the images often revolved around their view of the image's underlying category. For example, the image of the pop star Madonna and female runner sparked discussions about the underlying category of woman. Pregnant man and male model sparked conversations about the category of man.

Although this happened without any prompting on our part, it came as no surprise. Categories are the cognitive building blocks of our conceptual system. Categories enable us to sort the infinite stimuli with which we are bombarded daily, and enable us to make sense of the world. Research supports the view that categories are formed in people's minds around a prototype, or best example.[2] For instance, the wooden chair upon which I am sitting is prototypical of many people's idea of 'chair'. Other chairs are judged according to how closely they resemble our idea of a prototypical chair. A stuffed, frilly armchair is likely to be judged more prototypical than a wheelchair, but perhaps not as prototypical as my wooden chair. An electric chair, although having some chair qualities, may be judged as outside the category, in that the purpose of a chair, to provide a comfortable seat for a human, is violated in the extreme. Is it even a chair?

Thus, categories have fuzzy boundaries. Social categories (such as gender) are even fuzzier, and require work to maintain or redefine them. This work is vital, for without this capacity to make and maintain basic categories, our world view would dissolve into a chaotic jumble. In view of this, it not surprising that delineating the boundaries of basic social categories occupied so much of our young people's conversation.

During our analysis of the young people's conversations, it became apparent that the images were viewed in a variety of ways. There was some, but far from complete, consistency concerning whether an image was considered prototypical or not in relation to the underlying category. For example, male model and Buffy images were often, but not always, seen as good examples (prototypical), of the gender category they represented. Pregnant man was often, but not always, viewed as *not* prototypical – outside the category of 'man'. All 15 images image were viewed in more than one way and 75 per cent of the 15 images were viewed in three or more ways out of 5. Thus it appears that the relationship of an image to a category is largely in the eye of the beholder.

Coding young people's talk

It appeared that, when an image was judged to be prototypical, the category boundary was reinforced in young people's minds. An image outside the category also reinforced the category boundary by virtue of a negative example. In other instances, the boundaries become negotiable, arguable. One of five codes describing the image's status in relation to a category was assigned to the young people's talk about the images. These codes were: Prototypical, Outside, Contradictory, Ambiguous, or Off-the-Scale. The codes are described in Table 6.1.

Table 6.1 Is the image similar to category prototype?

	Prototypical	Outside	Contradictory	Ambiguous	Off-the-scale
Like prototype?	Image is similar to related category prototype.	Image is clearly outside category; unlike prototype.	Image elicits contested viewpoints within group, or within individual. Awareness of contradictory elements.	Visual uncertainty indicated: what does the image mean? Image is ambiguous in relation to prototype.	Image is so unlike previous conceptual-izations of category that it is threatening to wider belief system.
Effect on boundary of category	Category boundary maintained, reinforced. World view makes sense.	Category boundary is maintained and reinforced by negative example.	Some aspects of image are inside the category, others elements outside.	Is the category adequate for this image? What category? Category boundary not clear.	Image brings world view into question. World view is also defended.

Interviewee's talk was measured in terms of the number of (transcribed) text lines

A hypothesis evolved:

> How closely an image is judged to be similar to a category prototype influences the way young people think about the image.

This relationship is likely to be grounded in the kind of cognitive and social work needed to affirm or re-establish category boundaries. As these discussions occurred within the context of group discussion, we were tapping into the socially shared aspect of young people's category boundaries.

In psychological experiments, it is accepted that people's talk can provide a valid, if less extensive, account of their underlying thinking.[3] Following this, we analysed young people's talk (in other parts of the transcripts not already coded) according to different styles of thinking. There was a clear distinction in the young people's talk mapping on to 'open' and 'closed' thinking. Rokeach describes an open thinking system as capable of internal modification and development.[4] An open style of thinking has the potential to modify a conceptual system in order to deal with issues of increasing complexity, or internal contradictions. We coded examples of critical thinking, multiple interpretations, extensive moral reasoning, existential questioning, and indications of a willingness to rethink the currently held world view, as examples of an 'open' thinking style.

In contrast, young people's talk also gave evidence of a 'closed' thinking style, where the potential for modification and development of the thinking system is absent. Examples of closed thinking include: 'the world is as I thought', stereotyping, defensive manoeuvres, joking in a manner which dismisses or closes down, or regressive thinking (thinking showing emotional or cognitive traces of earlier developmental periods).

We were also concerned with identifying any spiritual dimension to young people's world view. As seen in earlier chapters, young people's sense of ultimate meaning was often organized around an idealized concept of 'family':

> Debbie: Like, there are two things in life you can't avoid and that's birth and death, and then this whole family bit in the middle.
>
> Nancy: I think they're all, like, family images because a baby is like the product of a family . . . and then the middle bit is, like, how you support your family and the end is, like, how, if you are lucky, you have your family round you, like when you are dying and stuff.

We looked for both transformative and formative spirituality, and for expressions of religious conviction. Young people's talk was coded in this way:

Table 6.2 Coding categories for young people's talk

Open Thinking	Closed Thinking
critical argument	'Just as I thought'
many interpretations	stereotyping
moral reasoning	closed down willingness to rethink world view
willingness to re-think world view	dismissive, defensive, 'not us'
	joking in order to close down
	childlike regression
Formative spirituality	
search for meaning	religion as meaningless
existential questioning	religion as 'sacred cow' for others
awe, delight, dread	
Transformative spirituality	
religion as meaningful	
regular spiritual practices	

Images considered prototypical

Three images, Madonna, male model and Buffy were often considered prototypical. For example, the young people would argue whether this particular image of Buffy or Madonna was a good example of the category of a woman.

Image: Buffy

Sibs: She looks a bit of a moron.

Don: Buffy.

Max: Funny nose.

Sibs: Pretty gormless as well.

Mary: Yeah she looks a bit confused.

Diana: No ... it's such a weird image but it's beautiful like a Barbie Doll.

Image: Madonna

Molly: That's Madonna, yeah.

Toni: That's a bit slappified, isn't it.

Molly: Yeah.

Toni: She's got her fishnets on with an ugly face and her big horrible hair and her bra. It don't look right. Nothing comes into my head. Clutching her fanny as well.

Bob: Nothing comes into your head? Do you like her pose or do you not like her pose?

Toni: Not really. It is a bit dirty. Boys would like that probably.

Bob: What comes into your head thinking of that?

Molly: Nothing.

Toni: Blonde bimbo.

Both Madonna and Buffy are perceived as the prototypical female, possessing 'looks not books'; she is a 'beautiful Barbie doll', a 'blonde bimbo'. Participants readily processed prototypical images and formed judgements about them.

Images viewed as prototypical tend to be immediately recognized. The Charles kissing Diana image was quickly identified and dismissed in this group interview. Here, the image (surprisingly) provided no doorway to discuss deeper issues such as betrayal or disappointment:

Megan:	Diana, and is it Prince Charles?
Samantha:	Getting married . . .
Jim:	That picture has no meaning for me, that's what I have to say about that one. I don't care about it at all.
Bob:	So you would like to get rid of the king and queen?
Jim:	Yep, hire a hit man.

Overall, 56 per cent of the young people's talk (measured in text lines) indicates open thinking; 44 per cent indicates closed thinking.

Where open thinking was in evidence in the group discussions, this took the form of critical arguments concerning issues such as royalty, commercialism and war. There was no mention of religious symbols as having significance to the young people. The most extensive mention of religion was as meaningful to others, to be defended for their sakes. The greatest amount of moral disgust (the strongest moral emotion) was expressed concerning prototypical images. It is as if a clear-cut category provides clear-cut moral sentiment, either positive:

> 'She (Madonna) is such a beautiful person inside and outside', 'that's definitely a positive image',

or negative:

> 'very cheesy', 'she's ugly, really minging', 'gross', 'she's a slagger', 'it's disgusting'.

In response to prototypical images that reinforce category boundaries, young people's moral reasoning was often *absolutist* (following Kant, that actions are inherently right or wrong) or *emotivist* (that moral imperatives are really statements of feeling).

In response to the task questions, where young people were active in choosing images, a greater range of implicit moral philosophies was apparent. In descending order of magnitude young people's moral reasoning showed:

● Intentionism (it is the motivation for the action that makes it moral or not);

● Utilitarianism (the outcome of the action is important, for example the greatest good or happiness for the greatest number); and

● Kantian reasoning (that actions are inherently right or wrong in themselves).

The most extensive comments about visual impact, colour and contrast were made concerning the chosen prototypical images. For example, concerning male model:

> I like the colour contrast and he looks a bit like George Clooney which is nice as well, but I really like the way he is sort of orange and the background is really blue; sets it off well. (Liz)

It may be that the ease of perceiving and processing the image leaves room for paying attention to the visual properties of the image per se. Producers of media images are undoubtedly aware that visual impact is maximized when the image is easily recognized, and where category boundaries are maintained. This is advantageous to producers who want to grab attention and entertain, but disadvantageous if open thinking is desired. Unfortunately, commercial success is more likely to be driven by the former rather than the latter. It is no secret that popular images often trade on this immediacy.

Finally, it is striking that discussions concerning prototypical images showed some features of fundamentalist styles of thinking: a degree of closed thinking, a fervent concern for right and wrong, strong moral revulsion, defending religion for the sake of others, and, in response to open-ended questions, absolutist moral reasoning.[5] It seems as if images which present 'the world as I know it', whose category boundaries are reinforced by the image, are accompanied by a more dogmatic mindset: the world is clear-cut.

Images perceived as outside the category

Four of the 15 images were often considered by a number of the young people as outside the category: Pregnant man, female runner, male model and newborn baby (Benetton).

Image: Female runner

She looks weird, she looks like she has four arms, she looks gay . . . it doesn't look normal. (Mark)

Image: Male model

Oscar: Joey posed for that . . .

Johanna: Sunburn.

Oscar: Ponce.

Bob: You like him, you like that one, smooth? . . . Is that a good example of a man or is that . . .

Oscar: It is not an average example of a man.

Bob: It is not average except in Hollywood or something?

Oscar: *This* is the average man [referring to Steve, with his Manchester t-shirt on].

Stewart: Below average.

Images perceived as outside the category tended to elicit curt discussions flavoured with sarcasm. In the results, 51 per cent of young people's talk indicated closed thinking; 49 per cent indicated open thinking.

Gender categories dominated these discussions, and these were rendered in highly traditional ways. Women have to be good looking. They can be strong, but not so strong that they look masculine. In the context of these group discussions, the young people were unforgiving concerning what they considered to be outside a social category.

Outside images were entirely negatively evaluated (the ratio of negative to positive evaluation text lines is 81 : 0). As with prototypical images, right and wrong, and likes and dislikes, were clearly demarcated.

Image: Anti-fur ad

Simon: She is a stupid whore to do that.

Mark: I think she is a rich thing.

Simon: . . . smack her in the face.

Mark: I [think] she should be killed and made into a skin coat . . . and . . . pee on her.

There was very little moral reasoning concerning these images, and the least extensive discussion evidencing any spirituality. Complaints about boredom, commercialism and the unrealism of the image were prevalent. There were no comments about the image's visual properties (colour, shape, contrast). As with prototypical images, outside images seem to serve as boundary reinforcers. But with outside images, the young people's thinking was even more closed. It appears that these images suggest a world so obviously clear-cut that deliberation is unnecessary. Outside images appear to beg to be dismissed by young people.

Contradictory images

Of the 15 images, 13 were considered 'contradictory', evidenced by some aspects of the image being regarded as inside the category, while other aspects were considered outside. Images perceived as contradictory cover a wide range of subject matter, including: newborn, Charles kissing Diana, the anti-fur ad, Madonna and Ali G on the cross. An image was considered contradictory either when an individual, or the wider group, pointed out contradictory elements.

Image: Madonna

Helen: I have a lot of respect for Madonna, but she looks like a slut.

Jasmine: No, I think she's good to do that.

Helen: I think she's great.

Image: Anti-fur ad

Mary: I hate people that shoot things.

Sibs: But I think that advert is silly.

Mary: But it takes 40 dumb animals to keep me alive . . . but a fur coat I can keep forever.

Sibs: . . . seems really brutal but it's probably not that bad.

Mary: It makes you seem like you don't know that you kill animals to make fur coats, but you know that, so you think about it anyway.

Don: I suppose it depends what the animal is. I mean if it's one that is a protected animal then that's bad, but if it's just one that, you know, because you eat animals.

Max: Did you see the one they made of hamsters? (laughter)

Sibs: No, I have to say that doesn't really – I just think of all the stupid people that threw red paint at the catwalk . . . And there are so many things in the world that are so much more important than a few fluffy animals, like children. There's 40 dumb children dying every day and nobody cares about them but they care about some stupid Siberian wolf.

Images perceived as contradictory elicited approximately four times more open than closed thinking.[6]

Discussions concerning these images revealed an intensity and richness as young people engaged in lengthy arguments. They sank their teeth into the battle, with fewer closing down, dismissive tactics. Critical argument and multiple interpretations predominated. Contradictory images elicited the most extended moral reasoning. Moral reasoning followed most commonly along non-absolutist utilitarian lines, closely followed by intentionist. Some of the most vehement moral revulsion was expressed over the commercial use of the two Benetton ads featuring a naked, bloody newborn baby and a man dying of AIDS.

Image: Man dying of AIDS

Noreen: That really is prostitution, that is horrible.

Bob: Could you explain why you . . .

Noreen: Because it's dying. He is in pain and it's Benetton and it's not fair.

Luke: . . . all about it.

Noreen: It really upsets me, it's just an advert and it's really bad.

Bridget: What do you think is happening there?

Noreen: This really ill guy and everybody is really upset and they are crying and it's a Benetton ad . . .

Verbalizations indicating formative spirituality far exceeded those pertaining to outside images, but were less extensive than in response to prototypical or ambiguous images. Argument and multiple interpretations predominated.

Ambiguous images

Of the 15 images, 11 were considered ambiguous by at least some young people. Young and old, man dying of AIDS, and forest fire were most frequently considered ambiguous, followed by the image of September 11th. With 11 images viewed as ambiguous, a wide range of subject matter was covered. An image was coded as ambiguous when the young people evidenced that they were not sure what the image *signified*. With these images, they had to ask questions and struggle to make sense of what they are seeing.

Image: Forest fire

Sarah: I think that looks a bit like heaven.

Izzy: Could look like fire, couldn't it?

Matt: Lava.

Izzy: I just didn't realize looking at it now, cos it kind of looks like light is shining through.

Sarah: Is it meant to be . . .?

Ambiguous images appear to immediately mean *something* to young people, but this meaning has to be discovered. This contrasts with the wholly abstract images presented in the pilot phase. Abstract art or hard-to-decipher photographs of natural objects elicited only cursory responses and were culled.

It is no surprise that throughout the group interviews young people were engaged with a degree of impression management. They were presenting to each other a 'cool' image of themselves which coincided with their concept of an ideal self. With ambiguous images, it seemed that these social rules were suspended. A door was opened to discussing deeper issues.

Nearly eight times more open than closed thinking was in evidence here, with 89 per cent of total thinking being 'open' with ambiguous images.

Non-absolutist moral reasoning was foremost. A rough version of utilitarianism prevailed, followed by intentionism. Indications of formative spirituality are in evidence in awe and wonder, dread and existential questioning in response to ambiguous images.

There was more than four times more extensive verbalization showing spiritual potential in relation to ambiguous images in comparison with the average of the four other image categories. Talk suggesting transformative spirituality (or talk of religion as meaningful) was a microscopic proportion of young people's conversation: 0.003 per cent of all talk coded as open thinking.

There were some remarks of an overtly religious nature. These were made by young people who identified themselves as Christian, who, interestingly, revealed their faith more fully in response to ambiguous images than overtly religious images.

Image: Forest fire

Luke: It's on fire.

Patrick: Fire, it's a volcano or something.

Luke: Yes, it is and there's the deer and they are goin' die, get out of the way . . . Bambi.

Amy: Oh I am going to cry.

Bob: You're going to cry.

Amy: Yes it's just really horrible and scary and like, is that actually a volcano or is it a fire?

Patrick: A volcano, it looks like a volcano because it looks too intense to be a fire. All the trees are up there. In a fire you don't get every tree and things.

Amy: So it's a volcano.

Patrick: It looks like a volcano.

Bob: Well, I want you to respond to the image in any sense whatever, to read whatever you read into it.

Amy: I don't know, it's almost kind of beautiful in like an amazing colourfying way.

Luke: So you have to look at it to see what it actually is because it's that many colours and that many, like, and you have to – and it's all that small, a very small picture.

Amy: It kind of speaks to me about God a lot when I see huge things like that, like a huge power of like a volcano, it kind of makes me think, well, cos that's kind of like, I don't know . . . kind of talks to me about God because God . . .

Luke: . . . than me and how much bigger is God than that . . .

The images seem to provide a gateway into a more complex world, a world that can inspire awe as well as dread.

Image: Young and old

Helen: It's a scary thing, isn't it, our parents who looked after us for so long and now she is looking after her mother, the roles are reversed . . . makes you think about your life right now, how you are going to age and scary . . . reflection on how you are going to be when you get to . . . it makes you think how will I be when I get to that [age].

Jasmine: It's a realization that we will actually get old because when you are young you don't think you will do but you are going to, so it's quite scary I suppose . . .

> Helen: It's not very comforting it's the whole what might happen when you get older . . .

The rough and tumble of joking, and defensive statements were still present, but so too was a willingness to rethink their prevailing world view. In fact, the Happy midi-narrative observed throughout this research was at times overtly challenged, as in the discussion above. Life was sometimes discussed in terms of irresolvable conflicts, or even in terms of bleak tragedy. The active condition, where participants were invited to select an image, or to group three images and tell a story about them, elicited the most direct statements about tragic (and unjust) aspects to the social world, or to life in general. The normal taboo on speaking about irresolvable unhappiness seemed to be lifted when young people were free to create their own stories, using media images as their raw material. If there is a silent, 'depressed' aspect to young people's world view (see Chapter 3), it was hinted at here.

Image: Forest fire

> Sarah: It is a good contrast between like the animals and not knowing what is going on and they are quite peaceful and . . .
>
> Matt: Not for much longer.
>
> Sarah: Yeah, exactly before they find out what is coming; and it is kind of tragic, like 'oh this really nice wildlife' [wild life, or wildlife?] and . . . red like blood kind of like death doesn't it.
>
> Izzy: Yeah.

We were surprised by these findings. In the piloting phase, it had been our expectation that the Salvador Dali painting of Christ, the Hubble telescope image of distant stars, *X-files* actors, Ali G on the cross, man dying of AIDS (upon whose face is superimposed the face of Jesus), and the image of Buffy the vampire slayer holding a stake might elicit evidence of spiritual quest (as is prevalent among Generation X-ers). This did not transpire. When it was pointed out that Jesus' face had been superimposed on the dying man, a typical response was: 'I don't care about that at all.' Even Buffy failed to ignite anything other than scorn (or admiration for her looks). While the subject matter of some ambiguous images clearly does matter to young people (the planet and the threat of ageing), our overall impression is that young people's formative spirituality was evoked by the process of *actively wrestling with the image*.

Off-the-scale images

Four images were perceived by some young people as 'off-the-scale'.

These included the Twin Towers, Charles kissing Diana, the anti-fur ad, and Munch's painting *The Scream*. These images seem to have been perceived by these young people to be so far outside the boundaries of everyday categories as to be threatening or incomprehensible.

Image: Twin Towers

Noreen: [It] scared me cos I was on the phone to my mum and she just said that 'Independence Day' had happened and like because she had just seen it on the news and she thought that the whole of New York had gone.

The images of September 11th were often anchored in 'homey' events: 'I got in and my Mum was on the phone', 'my Dad sat in front of the telly', 'I went to my Auntie's when I heard about it', using more childlike references to home life than anywhere else in the data collection. This 'regression' is all the more marked given that these were discussions within peer groups.

At the same time, extensive, critical discussions about the political and economic conditions surrounding September 11th opened up, along with musings on sudden death and injustice.

Grouping task

Yes. We chose pictures, [Twin Towers], [Gulf War] ... and they are all about sort of war, and they are all images of war. The first ones are the Twin Towers and the planes going into the Twin Towers, and it shows the sort of trigger of war and people's hatred for other people and the extent they go to, to practise that hatred. And there is a lot of smoke from this one [Gulf War] which is a recurring theme, where in fact more than half of the picture is like black smoke; but this shows what happens after the trigger of war when war is going on and normal people, like the chap in the middle, is just a normal bloke and he is drawn into war, and he is just looking out on it like it's normal. And so he has become numb to the awfulness of it, which should never happen ... the last picture ... shows like the result of war and all the fighting and how terrible it is. All so smoky and black. And it shows the pain of how terrible war is but also as all these children are running away screaming, all the soldiers are like walking around like there is nothing happening, like it's not bad at all. And like in the other photo it shows how they have become numb to it and how that is really terrible. (Diana)

Thinking seemed to move back and forth between open and closed directions, opening up discussion to encompass the enormity of events, and then hurrying back to safer territory. Given the shocking 'life and death' nature of these images (and the implicit reference to conflict between Islam and the West), it is surprising there were no references at all to religious themes, either to defend religion, dismiss or extol it. They simply did not arise. Off-the-scale images (although fewer in terms of range of images, so caution is needed in extrapolating results) seem to provide a door which can swing in both open and closed directions.

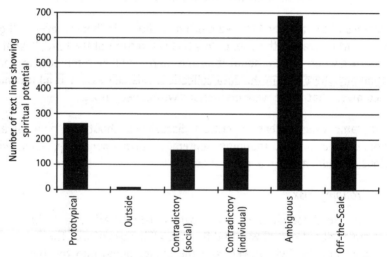

Figure 6.1 Formative spirituality (measured in text lines).

Comparisons between groups

Comparisons between groups on the basis of demographic differences reveal some conditions which we think are advantageous for eliciting open thinking and spirituality among young people.

Gender

It is well known that females show a greater propensity to overt spirituality than males. In response to the open-ended questions, all-male focus groups showed slightly less extensive formative spirituality than all-female groups

Table 6.3 Summary of category properties

	Type of thinking	Moral reasoning	Evaluations	Visual properties
Prototypical	Near equivalent amount open to closed thinking. Some critical argument. Religion not significant, but rigid, fundamentalist style.	Strong moral revulsion. Moral reasoning follows absolutist, emotive lines, but varies in active condition.	Black and white evaluations. Strong likes and dislikes. Boredom, commercialism, unrealistic.	Most awareness of visual elements; colour and dark/light contrast, composition. Visual more like an end in itself.
Outside	More closed than open thinking. No religious mention at all. Very little spiritual potential.	No moral reasoning.	More negative than positive. Boredom, commercialism, not realistic.	No mention of visual elements.
Contradictory	4 × more open than closed thinking. Critical argument most extensive, many interpretations, some spiritual potential.	Most extensive moral argument. Utilitarian thinking predominates, but varies more in active condition.	Negative (more often) and positive. Images considered most realistic.	Mid-range awareness of visual elements.
Ambiguous	8 × more open than closed thinking. Awe and wonder. Most spiritual potential. More 'significant' religious mention.	Utilitarian foremost, but of all image types, most varied lines of moral reasoning in both active and less active conditions	Positive (more often) and negative. No boredom or commercialism mentioned.	Second most extensive mention of visual elements: colour and dark/light contrast. Visual elements more like a doorway to thinking.
Off-the-scale	3 × more open than closed thinking, also regressive. thinking. *No* religious mention. Critical argument and willingness to subvert usual world view.	More absolutist and emotivist moral reasoning, varies in active condition.	Positive, strong impact.	Little mention of visual elements.

(comparisons control for the number of male to female focus groups). When including the active tasks, this trend reversed, and all-male focus groups showed twice as much formative spirituality, including more extensive reference to religion, in comparison with the all-female groups. It seems that the active tasks allow for the initiative and freedom in which it is possible, or socially acceptable, for males to express their spirituality. Mixed-gender groups, however, showed proportionally more formative spirituality and mention of religion as meaningful (admittedly a tiny proportion in text lines!) in both conditions.

Christian and non-Christian groups

All-Christian groups showed four times more extensive formative spirituality in comparison to non-Christian groups. Non-Christian groups talked less frequently about religion, and when they did mention it, it was mostly in terms of religion as meaningless. However, mixed groups showed slightly more formative spirituality than either. Reference to religion as meaningful was made most extensively within mixed Christian and non-Christian groups (an evangelistic campaign among the Christians for the benefit of the non-Christians?). The lesson here is: mix Christians with non-Christians and *all* benefit.

Age, race, employment

The younger focus groups (comprising young people 16-years-old and younger) showed only 56 per cent open thinking, while the older groups (18+) showed 76 per cent open thinking. At least some of the older groups contained a greater mix of ages. Mixed rather than homogeneous groups, comprising students, employed and unemployed, also showed more open thinking.

Race shows similar trends, in that mixed-race groups showed more open thinking in comparison to all-White groups.

Numbers in focus groups

Smaller focus groups (with 5 members and below) showed lower ratios of open : closed thinking than groups with the reputedly optimal focus group number (between 6 and 12 participants). These optimally sized groups showed nearly twice as much open: closed thinking. There were two groups (with over 13 participants) with an even more favourable open: closed ratio, but the small number of cases here makes any generalizations unwise.

Academic or youth group setting

The most noticeable difference resulting from the setting of the focus groups is the prevalence of jokes told in youth club settings! Youth club settings also generated marginally more potential for spirituality, but overall, little difference in ratio of open : closed thinking (both youth clubs and academic settings showed 65 per cent open thinking). This is interesting given that the academic setting usually has a higher average level of education than the youth club setting, but this educational difference made no discernible impact. Fun, play and creativity are not optional extras, they invoke young people's Ideal as key virtues in the world view.

Summary

To our surprise, we found that young people's spirituality was evoked not so much through transient experiences of the Ideal (as might have been expected, for example, through high-stimulus clubbing experiences), but most strongly as young people engaged with the Actual through culturally iconic and advertising images of the social world. This was especially the case if the images were endowed with an element of ambiguity. Ambiguous, rather than traditional, or even 'alternative', religious images, have the most potential for eliciting open thinking, formative spirituality and talk about religion (of which only a minuscule proportion suggested transformative spirituality).

It must be remembered that ambiguous images had this effect within the context of the whole research design, which included discussion of 15 images, each of which was perceived in different ways by different people. It is not at all certain that presenting 'ambiguous' images to young people as a contrived technique would have the desired effect. They seem to be equipped with a homing device designed to pick up contrivance. In fact, each type of image serves a different purpose in enabling young people to wrestle with the building blocks of their world view. The impact may be collective: ambiguity may be ineffective without a context of some clear-cut, anchoring categories.

The task questions intensified open thinking, a greater variety in lines of moral reasoning, and a willingness to subvert the usual Happy midi-narrative. The task questions were especially important for males. Under these conditions, the all-male groups atypically exceeded the all-female groups in talk indicating formative spirituality. (Mixed-gender groups exceeded both single sex groups.)

We conclude with some thoughts drawing on the interesting work of Semir Zeki[7] on art and the visual brain. Zeki says that visual art serves, in part, similar functions to the visual brain: to represent the constant, lasting, essential and enduring features of objects and surfaces, in order to allow us to construct knowledge of the outside world. Thus vision is an *active* process in which the brain in its quest for knowledge about the visual world discards, selects and compares information, and thus generates the visual image in the brain. Zeki says that this is a process remarkably similar to what a visual artist does. Visual artists have long known that this is their role: to construct and to reconstruct how we 'see' the world.

Great art, in neurological terms, comes closest to showing as many facets of reality as possible, rather than mere, fleeting appearance. Ambiguity is the characteristic of great paintings, which allow for, and invite, multiple, equally valid interpretations – thus telling us *more* about life. Ambiguity is not just vagueness, but the certainty of many different possibilities.

I leave the last word here on the spiritual potential of ambiguity to Schopenhauer:

> Something, and indeed the ultimate thing, must always be left
> over for the imagination to do.[8]

Theological reflection

Images proved to be the most effective of the three art mediums in triggering young people's imagination. Soap operas and films enabled young people to think about how they might have responded in a similar situation. Music amplified what they were already feeling, but images, particularly ambiguous images, sparked imagination. One of the images used was of deer drinking from a pool in a forest clearing set against a golden sky – the young people wondered whether the deer in the forest were at risk of fire, or whether they were bathed in golden sunlight. The uncertainty of such images required mental effort, and gave the young people an opportunity to speculate on the true nature of the situation.

We see this imagination-provoking quality of images deployed in Scripture. Isaiah and Ezekiel both used symbolic actions: Isaiah, at one point, entirely in the nude (Isaiah 20.1–6), and Ezekiel with a dramatic portrayal lasting more than a year (Ezekiel 4.1–8). Elisha used a bow and arrow (2 Kings 13.15–19), and Ahijah tore up his cloak to get the message across (1 Kings 11.30). Jeremiah used a variety of props to 'image' rather than verbalize his message: a loincloth (13.1–14), pottery (18.1; 19.1–5), goblets of wine (25.15–36), stones (43.8–13), scrolls (51.62–64) and yokes (27.1 – 28.17). Jesus used a child to illustrate the nature of the kingdom of Heaven (Matthew 18.3), a fig tree to illustrate the nature of faith (Matthew 21.18–22), and a coin to illustrate the nature of good citizenship (Matthew 22.21).

All of these images work either to capture people's attention or else to fire their imagination. The common point to all of them is that they are not immediately explicable; they all need further explanation in order to be understood. These symbols are intended to provoke a response rather than to clarify a situation. No Israelite would have, immediately, known what to do in response to Isaiah walking around in the nude. They would have felt startled and challenged by his behaviour and wondered what point he was making. Isaiah was creating an image that would require some effort to find out and understand what he meant by it. This ambiguity is not simply vagueness, but rather a presentation of the unknowable majesty of God and a realization of a range of possibilities in response.

This richness is embedded within the heart of the Christian faith. Ambiguity is a reflection of the mystery that is part of the essential nature of God. The term 'mystery' appears three times in the Gospels, twenty-one times in Paul's letters, and four times in Revelation. Ambiguity is built into the Christian belief structure, enabling free choice and a freely given response.[9] This ambiguity is illustrated in Jesus' use of parables. Parables are verbal pictures designed to provoke curiosity rather than answer questions. It was only when Jesus was alone with his disciples that he explained what he actually meant.

Jesus' miracles are one area where the interpretation of Scripture can gloss over the role of ambiguity in enabling people to respond freely to the message of Christ. The miracles are always performed in *response* to faith rather than to create, or coerce, faith. When Jesus was in his home town, people had closed minds as to who Jesus was; thus, they had no faith, and because they had no faith, Jesus could do no miracles (Mark 6.5).

At times, the mission of the Church is to make the truths of God clear, simple and accessible. At other times the mission of the Church is to spark people's curiosity and stimulate their interest. This then draws people into a shared context where they can explore further. The research suggests that the use of ambiguous images is a good way to make young people inquisitive and provoke a response. As with images used in Scripture, these then provide a bridging opportunity for further explanation. They reflect the mysterious and ultimately unknowable nature of God, triggering wonder and imagination. Ambiguity is at the heart of any faith, and belief is a balancing act between knowing and not knowing:

'I believe, help my unbelief.' (Mark 9.24)

PART THREE:
IMPLICATIONS FOR YOUTH WORK AND THE WIDER CHURCH

We hope you have found the first two parts of this book intriguing, but what does it all mean in terms of how we do church and youth work?

In the next three chapters we set out some of the implications of our findings in terms of principles for church life and youth work practice. We have avoided prescriptions of 'what to do' – things are more complex than that. Instead we offer some general principles and signposts to resource ministry in your specific context.

In Chapter 7 Bob and Sara discuss implications for youth work, and in Chapters 8 and 9 Bishop Graham Cray reflects on implications for the Church.

7

The world view of Generation Y: Implications for Christian-based youth work

Prior mission

The distance between the world views of the Church and Generation Y leads us to conclude that *prior mission* to young people is now required. *Prior mission* is about encouraging imagination, going beyond clichéd symbols or catchphrases, and allowing young people to articulate their own questions.[1] Prior mission starts with the reality of who young people are, and the questions they are asking. This will involve a primary focus on who young people want to become rather than what young people should be doing – this focus is on identity formation rather than moral decision making. We argue that a focus on 'being' rather than 'doing' will link more easily with the ideal self that the young person wants to become. The popular arts can be used to draw out from young people their ability to imagine, explore and identify the person they want to become. This, we believe, is a necessary first step in reaching out to Generation Y.

In our post-Christian age, this process of 'drawing out' from young people is the necessary prior work needed to enable them to recognize, understand and then connect with their own basic, formative spirituality. This process cannot be rushed, and will sorely test Christian propensities to leap to the correct answer! Formative spirituality needs a genuinely unpressured space – of indeterminate length – in order for an authentic movement from formative spirituality towards a committed transformative spirituality to occur. Then, the possibility of God may be acknowledged, and ultimately we hope, encountered through Jesus Christ.

Formative vs transformative spirituality

The Church needs to distinguish between young people's basic formative spirituality (a raised awareness of relationality with self, other, the universe) and a committed, transformative spirituality. Young people's instinctive search for identity and understanding cannot be assumed to be evidence of an unspoken interest in a transcendent God. We argue that the allegedly widespread phenomenon of eclectic spiritual seeking among young people, burgeoning on the back of a decline in religion, is illusory. Rather, we found that young people's spirituality needs to be understood in terms of the very basic, *formative* spirituality, which for the young people we interviewed is felt to be sufficient for their well-being. In a similar vein, Smith and Denton[2] argue that very few American youth under the age of 18 are interested in or actively pursue an eclectic spiritual-but-not-religious personal quest. A hypothetical illustration may help:

> Two people get knocked off their bikes and have near-death experiences. One person thinks he is lucky and resolves to live life to the full. The second thinks he is protected by God and starts going to church as a result.

We think young people in England have the kind of world view which makes them more likely to respond as the first person, rather than as the second, in our illustration. There is no automatic transformative spirituality built into the experience of getting knocked off a bicycle, just as there is no transformative spirituality inherent within a clubbing experience, watching films or viewing cultural icons. The point to recognize is that it is what a young person takes *into* a situation that shapes how they understand the experience. If someone talks of worshipping God on a clubbing night out, then it is likely that they already have a framework of Christian understanding within which they interpret the experience.

Formative spirituality is not an automatic bridge to transformative spirituality. The fact that a young person is in the process of working out what they consider to be important is not evidence, in itself, that they are responding to the hidden qualities of God evident through creation (Romans 1.20). It may be nothing more than wish fulfilment on behalf of the Christian constituency to read into a young person's natural process of learning, self-development and search for meaning, a hunger for God.

The challenge for Christian youth work is thus to discover how formative spirituality can become transformative spirituality. With some young people there may be an overlap and the former will move effortlessly towards the latter. With others, there may be the potential to build on the formative so that it can be developed into the transformative. With yet others, the formative may lead young people away from the transformative, because they need to work out for themselves their own values, and this could actually make them turn away from a religious faith.

It is true that clubbing, fantasy and action films and music might engender for young people a concept of an Ideal: an experience of exciting, creative possibility in which everyone is happy. However, there is no reason why a young person should assume that the feeling of well-being engendered by a familiar piece of music, or the imagination triggered by a good film or the fun of a good night out are in any way evidence of there being something more to life than the immediate and the experiential. There is no reason why Christians should assume a young person's experience of a happy Ideal will automatically become a part of a transformative spirituality. These popular arts on their own *do not* catapult young people into a search for God. These 'good times' are an end in themselves. This does not mean these experiences are trivial. Rather they are *key* to a Generation Y world view in which this world and all life is meaningful as it is. Young people's undergirding Happy midi-narrative is a celebration of this world, rather than an anticipation of the next.

The young people we interviewed were not dissatisfied with their lives. We found no evidence of them looking for a transcendent 'something more'. Yet inherent within much Christian youth ministry is the assumption that young people do have an innate need to look for some greater purpose and meaning beyond day-to-day life. The assumption that young people have a felt need for God (however indistinct), provides a rationale for Christian youth ministry because it sees itself as uncovering and then meeting this need. This approach does not sit comfortably with either youth ministry or with youth work. It does not sit comfortably with youth ministry because an emphasis on a theology of sin and the need for salvation might not offer young people adequate opportunities to explore their place in the world (prior mission). It sits uncomfortably with youth work because the principles of informal education in youth work are to do with transparency and openness. To use Christianity as a hidden agenda that can be produced once a young person has 'realized their need' is disingenuous. Our suggestion drawn from the research is this: 'Relax, present the gospel simply – as it is – it is good news.' Young people are not going to be hostile towards a Christian faith that they know little about, and hence the fact that Christianity is not talked about with young people might often be more to do with the hesitancy of the youth worker than the hostility of the young people. There is a new Generation Y young person emerging who does not know, and who may never have heard, the basic Christian story.

Our research suggests that those engaged in youth work and ministry need to think in terms of connecting with the hopes and aspirations of young people, to address the ideal self they want to become. For the young people we interviewed, popular arts offered an opportunity for them both to express and to explore who they saw themselves to be. Each of the three artistic mediums did this in a different way. Music tended to amplify and to confirm what young people were thinking or feeling anyway; stories tended to contextualize their personal experiences; and images tended to challenge and provoke imagination. The young people chose music to echo what they were feeling. Music was used to make a situation familiar or fun. These situations then became particular, distinctive and exclusive to the young people. Stories, and in particular soap operas, tended to be listened to in multigenerational family groups and hence provided a more shared, inclusive experience. The young people would read themselves into the plot and imagine what they might do in a similar situation. Images required effort from the young people to work out what was meant by the pictures. This meant that images could be used to trigger reflection on some basic assumptions and categories through which the young people interpreted the pictures.

We now return to our initial research question. From the outset, we wondered what young people's spirituality looks like, and whether the popular arts could resource the Church to 'do' theology in meaningful ways. Can the popular arts help the Church regain an authentic relationship with young people? Our answer to this question is a *qualified* yes: While experiences of the Ideal via the popular arts do not lead to a transformative spirituality, we did find that when the popular arts engage with the Actual, and unveil *real life*, a connection can be made with young people's basic existential questions. With these points in mind, the following sections contain general principles for using the popular arts in youth work and youth ministry.

Ambiguity and formative spirituality

We found that images of the social world that were visually ambiguous to the beholder fostered an active search for understanding. Conversation among young people opened up in a unique way as they tried to work out what the picture meant. This openness at times evidenced wonder, dread, awe and delight. We glimpsed in these instances a sense of relationality (with the others, self, the universe), which we describe as formative spirituality.

We suggest that the youth worker collects a large number of potentially ambiguous images of the social and natural world. You can download interesting images from various web sites, as well as trawl through magazines and newspapers. We identified ambiguity in an image when our interviewees showed they were trying to make sense of what the image was about: 'Is that a forest fire, or a sunset?' 'Is that a mirror, or is she looking at herself when she is older?'

Purely abstract art did not produce an active search for meaning, and these images were culled during the piloting phase. Images ambiguous to the beholder seem to have potentially decipherable, multiple meanings to young people. The young people's unique response to ambiguous images occurred in our study within the context of their responses to a whole range of other images and stimuli from the popular arts. We are not certain that ambiguity would work as an isolated 'technique'.

'Layering' popular arts

Young people are constantly immersed in an intermingling and layering of the popular arts. Words, images and music are combined in public social spaces, such as cafés or pubs, the jukebox blends with conversation, while television and video games permeate the atmosphere. Cinema blends dialogue, music and moving image. Clubbing is an intense symphony of music, movement, lights and projected images.

Churches also employ different media, but often only in a sequential manner. For example, a sermon (word) is followed by a hymn (music), which is followed by symbol (the bread and the wine), followed by a time of silence when visual images in stained-glass windows or banners become salient. The Church can learn from the contemporary blending and layering of media. Youth workers, too, can go beyond the Church's usual serial presentation when seeking to further young people's spiritual journey. As with ambiguous images, layering the different media provides a range of contexts, which allows for multiple and rich interpretations.

The essence of liturgy is an appropriate blending of music, word and image. This layering is beautifully achieved in some of the best alternative worship practices. In a similar way, the popular arts can be used to draw young people *further* along their spiritual journey. The various alternative worship practices, such as Grace, Revive, Holy Joes, LOPE and Epicentre and others, provide many fertile examples of this being done well.[3]

In these few examples the point to note is that each media form expands and deepens the others. This is illustrative of the rich, mysterious, never ending, process of knowing God. Of course, a delicate balance needs to be struck where each media enhances the other through subtle dialogue and interplay, avoiding the extremes of cacophony or stimuli overload. Overload can leave young people impressed by the imagery but with no idea of what it was meant to be about.

The *Mission-shaped Church* report and Fresh Expressions[4] initiative argues that a 'mixed economy church' is what is needed in the new cultural context we find ourselves in. One size no longer fits all. Parish churches and traditional models of ministry and church are to be encouraged and developed, but alongside these we need a whole set of 'fresh expressions' of (emerging) churches. Examples talked about include youth congregations, network churches, alternative worship, base communities, cell churches, new monastic orders, traditional church plants, café churches, multiple and midweek congregations, church in school, and so on.

Telling the story

While we argue that it is imperative to provide a genuinely free incubation space for formative spirituality, youth ministry seeks to go further and to communicate the Christian faith explicitly. How can this be done sensitively? Far from exhibiting a postmodern eschewal of all narratives, young people's world view via the popular arts takes a narrative form: the Happy midi-narrative. We observed young people buzzing over stories. Stories, such as those in *EastEnders*, are a great resource for problem solving, identity formation and social interaction. The Bible can offer a parallel resource for young people's identity formation – the Proverbs, for example, offer accessible aphorisms which may resonate with young people's situation. The young people talked of watching soap operas with their family, and of listening to music on their own. This distinction may mean that a shared interest in story rather than a shared love of music is, initially, an easier way for the youth worker to make contact with young people.

Recall that our young people did not evidence a rebellion or hostility against the faith. The Christian faith often has little relevance simply because it is largely unknown. Therefore, rather than giving their own experience in order to authenticate a gospel message of which young people are not even aware, youth ministers can use Scripture directly to create dialogue and discussion. Using layering and dialogue avoids force-feeding. It provides the resource of the gospel narrative intertwined with music, images and movement. Layering enables youth to colonize the story, and unpack its implications in their own way.

Facilitating a deep religious knowing

Ah, you may rebut, layering the story leaves the work of understanding its significance too much to chance. Young people may distort it, or tear it to shreds!

We argue that this is a chance the Church has always taken. In the context of worship services, deep religious knowing has always depended upon bringing together both 'head' and 'heart'. In the language of cognitive psychology, two cognitive subsystems are involved in religious knowing: a word-based system (to do with language and linear thinking), and an implicational system (to do with latent, dense meanings not easily translated into language). It is the ability to use *both* these different cognitive subsystems *at the same time* that seems to reflect that distinctly human phenomenon of consciousness: we can reflect on our thoughts and experiences as one cognitive system 'talks' to another. When cross-talk between the word-based system and the deeper implicational system occurs, both head and heart are moved in such a way that the totality is greater than the sum of the parts.[5]

In this vein, evangelical, charismatic, catholic and liberal approaches have different emphases, but each orientation both provides a word-based framework (through liturgy, sermons, or testimonies) and engages the implicational system through music, symbols, movement, sacraments, or speaking in tongues. The richer and more layered the worship experience is, whatever the theological orientation, the more likely it will feed a deep, transformative religious knowing, engaging both 'head' and 'heart'.

It is the potential for 'cross-talk' between the two subsystems that enables a deep religious knowing.[6] This is a creative process, which occurs *within* the individual. Hence it is deeply personal. To misunderstand this, and to insist on a homogenized entrée into the Christian faith is to miss out on *the greater thing*, the potential for cross-talk between the word-based and implicational subsystems in religious knowing. Thus layering story, music, image, and movement enriches the power of each through the surrounding contexts. This potential for multiple layers of interpretation is precisely why we are never done reading the Bible.

Challenging assumptions in young people's world view

Youth workers can also use the popular arts to help young people become more self-critical of their own world view. We noted a lack of any wider political awareness in our sample of young people. This was shown in some basic assumptions which they make about the world:

- Life is a level playing field. Life is basically OK.
- Family and friends are always there to support you.
- Be yourself. Allow others to be themselves. This will add up to a collective happiness.

We also noted a recurrent contradiction in young people's talk about the popular arts, a contradiction for which they found no resolve: commercialism offers choice which is integral to the 'life world' represented by the Happy midi-narrative, however it then destroys originality.

Commercialism was seen as the 'enemy within' for both music production and clubbing. For example, music needs to have an 'edge' in order for it to become popular, and hence commercially successful. However, as soon as it becomes commercially successful it loses the edge that made it popular in the first place. A further case in point: clubs that were throbbing with hundreds of young people at the time of our data collection, are now, at the time of writing, closing down. Clubbing, like the genres of music which come and go, has proved ephemeral.

The copious amounts of money needed to sustain immersion in the popular arts requires substantial earning power. We observed that young people, captives to this consumerist cycle, tended to overlook the structural inequalities created by the commercial world which both feeds them and feeds off them. Young people need to be encouraged to explore the limitations of the Happy midi-narrative in the face of injustice and tragedy.

Critique of the Christian mindset: Redemptionitis

Young people's use of the popular arts to celebrate life, to enjoy relationships and community highlights certain imbalances within the Christian mindset. We need to listen to this implicit critique, and to face the flaws in the outworking of our faith. We too need to become self-critical concerning the accretions over the centuries to the Christian world view. Young people consider that the Church is eternally set in its ways. They will be astonished to discover that Christians are willing to face change! Fresh expressions of church which seek to wrestle free of these accretions will come as a welcome surprise.

Young people's celebration of life contrasts starkly with a Church that traditionally has focused on impulse control, targeting sins such as greed, lust or aggression as the prime means of fashioning obedience. Granted, these sins were great problems for hierarchically based traditional societies. Most of humanity was crushed under oppressive hierarchies, and religion in traditional cultures did help to limit some of the worst excesses of violence and sexual aggression (while legitimating others). In that earlier context, religion 'worked', at least to a degree. How well is it working now?

Impulse control ends up with a focus on 'doing' and obedience to ethical norms. The legacy for youth ministry of Christian preoccupation with duty and obedience is that youth ministers adopt some of the worst work habits of church leaders – chief among which is a tendency to overwork. The idea that working long hours is the unavoidable and the only way of expressing Christian commitment can leave both youth ministers and church leaders tired, stressed and resentful. Youth ministers are ideally placed to tap into the Happy midi-narrative of the emerging Generation Y. This will not happen, though, if what youth ministers end up doing and what young people end up hearing is nothing more than a thinly disguised form of duty and obligation. An unwritten code of commitments and responsibilities is bad news for youth work, draining energy and spontaneity out of hard-won relationships. There are too many youth ministers and church leaders who are constantly overworked, tired and stressed. They may want to show an open-handed love and respect to others, but they are not always so good at extending the same courtesy to themselves. To say that they are simply not managing their time well is not an adequate explanation.

Youth work is only as good as its underpinning theology. Unremitting hard work, busyness and duty are the baseline for youth work practice. This emerges out of a muddled understanding of doctrine. Doctrine shapes behaviour in the same way that ideas affect actions. This spiritualization of busyness comes out of what we call 'redemptionitis'. Redemptionitis is what happens when the Incarnation of Jesus is focused on to the exclusion of the doctrines of creation and eschatology. Creation and redemption provide interlocking and overlapping themes. Creation offers possibility and initiative, while redemption offers conclusion, judgement and decision; each echoes the other and each needs the other to provide a coherent whole. The fact that God created the world and saw that it was good (Genesis 1.10) is the ultimate affirmation – life in all its abundance (John 10.10). The fact that God redeemed the world through Jesus Christ sets up the ultimate challenge – denial of self to follow Jesus (Mark 8.34). A message offering creation and redemption together offers reconciliation and grace.[7] It is God's particular word of grace and judgement.[8] The danger is that a message that talks only of God's revelation through the Incarnation will place too great an emphasis on morality and duty. Young people are finding their place in the world, and will appreciate acceptance and welcome (as embodied in the idea of grace) from adults. Equally though, young people, with the confidence expressed by some of the interviewees, will appreciate advice and suggestions, even challenge (as embodied within the idea of judgement), from adults.

The appeal of redemptionitis teaching is that it is clear and direct. It offers security, order and purpose, and asks for morality, honesty, kindness and concern in return. It is more immediate than a message of grace and acceptance that seems to ask for nothing in return and can appear more abstract and harder to grasp. The focus is on activism rather than on reflection. The idea that what is important is what someone does rather than what they are is attractive in its accessibility. It is particularly appealing to the youth minister wanting to build bridges between believing church congregations and unchurched young people. There seems to be a lack of hypocrisy in the idea that what will judge someone is what they do rather than what they say they will do – 'You will know them by their fruits' (Matthew 7.20). Redemptionitis is attractive because it lets people know exactly what is expected of them – the appeal of WWJD (What would Jesus do?) is a case in point. It provides people with safe spaces that let them know exactly what they need to do and where they stand. For example, the Silver Ring Thing is a sexual abstinence programme designed to appeal to twenty-first-century teenagers and offer them protection from the destructive effects of America's sex-obsessed culture.[9] The attraction of the Silver Ring Thing initiative is that it is a clear, direct and obvious way to prove a commitment as a Christian. The issue is not virginity in and of itself, but virginity as an identity-marker for a Christian.

However, redemptionitis is ultimately destructive. If much is expected from people to whom much is given (1 Corinthians 4.2), then it is easy for an understanding of grace to slip into a sense of compulsion. The Christian is given the ability (through grace) rather than the obligation (through duty) to be obedient. The challenge is to imitate God (Ephesians 5.1) and to follow the example of Christ (1 Corinthians 11.1); however, this idea of obedience can easily become a sense of obligation. This then becomes not an invitation to a celebration, but a chance at progression and improvement. Eventually such a message disintegrates the gospel's meaning because it is no longer good news. If the gospel is authenticated by what people do rather than by what they believe and are, then the pressure is on the individual to get things right. Safe spaces become traps and people end up feeling guilty if they are not living up to what is expected of them.

This is the danger within the idea of 'relational youth work', which can leave the youth ministers feeling under pressure to do it all on their own. Youth ministers can be left feeling guilty if they are not spending huge amounts of their own time building individual relationships with young people outside the church. The phrase 'incarnational' youth work, common in youth ministry parlance, can also put subliminal pressure on people. Incarnational youth work appears to be asking the youth minister to act as the face of God to young people. If the keyword is 'authenticity' and the medium is the message,[10] then there is a lot of pressure put on the individual Christian to get it right.

> I can never be so confident of the authenticity of my witness that I can know that the person who rejects my witness has rejected Jesus. I am witness to him who is both utterly holy and utterly gracious. His holiness and his grace are as far above my comprehension as they are above that of my hearer.[11]

We argue that the Church's ethos of hierarchy and regulated behaviour sits uncomfortably with a networked, technologically literate, communication-aware Generation Y. It may also distort for young people the central Christian message of grace. A fluid network of relationships is the normal milieu for young people. Relationships, rather than rule following, form the basis of young people's morality (happiness for self and other). In comparison with the hierarchical model of social organization, a networked model may in fact be more conducive to the relationship dynamics that Jesus engendered among the disciples and intended for the Church. Youth have something to teach us in this regard.

This research is challenging the Church to take its own theology no less seriously than a Generation Y young person might take his or her place in the world. A youth minister is in the dreams business, helping young people to become the person they have it inside them to be. This requires creativity, care and imagination. It isn't going to happen if the youth minister is exhausted. Youth ministry is hard enough without youth ministers being made to feel that they are betraying some theological ideal if they are tired, crabby or out of sorts. When Jesus talked about faith the size of a grain of mustard seed being able to move mountains (Matthew 17.20), he was not suggesting that people get out their spades and start digging. According to the parable of the workers in the vineyard, however hard anyone works, everyone ends the day with the same amount (Matthew 20.1–16). The book of Ephesians presents the Church as God's masterpiece of reconciliation and a pilot scheme for the redeemed universe. However, this is a work of grace and not of effort and energy.

Transformed lives

To earn the right to have young people in our churches, both inherited and fresh expressions of church need to demonstrate the reality of transformed lives. To young people, an ideal self is centred on healthy relationships.

Young people believe that they should be treated as persons in their own right in the context of healthy relationships. In this respect young people appear to start out from a more psychologically resourced baseline than previous generations. We suggest this is due at least in part to the 'authoritative parenting style', which has become normative in the West. With the authoritative parenting style, there is a degree of reciprocity in give–and–take relations between parent and child. Authoritative parenting, which is warmly supportive yet also demanding, has reliably demonstrated the healthiest identity and achievement outcomes for offspring.[12] As we contemplate our desire to bring young people into the Church, we need to ponder the well-known dilemma faced by parents: Do we try to force young people to become *like us*? Or do we freely resource them become all they can be, trusting that this process will lead them – beyond us – towards God?

Given this expectation of reciprocal relationships (whatever experience a young person has had at home), hierarchical church practice seems 'backwards' in comparison to young people's psychologically informed goals. Why would a young person thus endowed with expectations of healthy relationship wish to sit in regimented pews in a cold stone building, passively taking instruction on how to live?

In earlier eras, it was sufficient to fulfil one's given social role. In that social context, church life based on hierarchical behaviour was appropriate, even necessary. Now it seems a backwards step. No longer do the social processes of inherited church provide the social learning which will equip people to live Christian lives in the contemporary context.[13]

Youth work as ethical practice

If we understand youth work as primarily an ethical endeavour, we can leave behind a redempionitis-informed emphasis on 'doing outreach' from a sense of duty and obligation, and embrace ideas of transformation over time by grace. We argue that a focus on character (who the young person is) will link more easily with the ideal self that the young person wants to become, and provide the Church with a focus of mission it is more able to achieve.

The youth work mission of the Church is an ongoing process of reflection and self-examination starting with the young person-as-is in the process of becoming the young person-as-could-be. It is this process of becoming that is described by Aristotle as ethics. The appeal of using Aristotle's ethics to understand how the Church can work with young people is that Aristotle describes the human condition in a way with which youth work can connect. In the *Nichomachean Ethics*,[14] Aristotle wrote that there is a fundamental contrast between man-as-he-happens-to-be and man-as-he-could-be-if-he-realized-his-essential-nature (i.e. human good or the human happiness, known as *eudaimonia*). A central plank of youth work is to enable young people to ask and answer the central questions about themselves: 'What sort of person am I?' 'What kind of relationships do I want to have with myself and others?' and 'What kind of society do I want to live in?'[15]

Ethics is the discipline that enables people to understand how they make the transition from the actual to the ideal self. According to Aristotle, happiness is found in exercising the moral virtues. For the Church, happiness is found in realizing the love of God revealed in Jesus Christ. Viewing youth work as an ethical activity takes the focus away from doing and places the emphasis on character formation. It is in this process of becoming that the movement from the Actual to the Ideal, Wright's world-view questions, and the aims of youth work and ministry meet. This avoids the mishmash of relativism inherent in the philosophy of individual rights that currently underpins youth and community work. Youth workers need some basis for resolving the ethical issues they encounter.[16] Viewing youth work as an ethical activity avoids what MacIntyre calls 'emotivism', where all evaluative judgements have become nothing more than expression of preference, attitude or feeling.[17] This is paralleled by Bloom's concept of 'religion as opinion', that following a great epistemological struggle, religion has been confined to the realm of opinion.[18] Understanding youth work as ethics frees the Church from being boxed in by this nettled question of 'truth'. Youth work as ethics, rather than morality, is free to ask the question: what sort of person is the young person going to become?

Summary of implications

- Young people's undergirding Happy midi-narrative is a celebration of this world, rather than the next.
- Prior mission allows young people to articulate their own existential questions about the person they want to become.
- Experiences of the happy Ideal via the popular arts do not automatically lead to a transformative spirituality, but when the popular arts engage with *real life*, a connection can be made with young people's questions.
- Ambiguous images can connect with young people's formative spirituality.
- Layering the different media provides a range of contexts, which allow for multiple, rich interpretations.
- Keep telling the gospel story, but in a layered way.
- Deep religious knowing occurs when both head and heart are moved in such a way that the totality is greater than the sum of the parts.
- Youth workers can use the popular arts to help young people become more self-critical of their own world view.
- Christians also need to be self-critical: redemptionitis is an overemphasis on the death of Jesus to the exclusion of the doctrines of creation and eschatology.
- The Church's ethos of hierarchy and behaviour control sits uncomfortably with Generation Y, whose normal milieu is a fluid network of relationships.
- Youth work as ethics is free to ask the question: what sort of person is the young person going to become?

Taking things further

A student from the Centre for Youth Ministry arranged a service using the four elements: earth, wind, fire and water. For earth, there were trays of earth spread out on the floor. People could write things they wanted to confess in the soil and then wipe them away with their hand. For wind, a big sheet was suspended between two pillars with fans behind so that it was rippled by the air. People wrote their prayers on to an acetate, which was then projected onto the sheet. Fire was represented by candles for prayer, and water was poured over people's hands as symbol of asking the Holy Spirit to refresh them. The use of multiple symbols fits well with the principle of layering described above, and was successful in engaging young people in worship.

We have chosen to focus on the principles for youth work and youth ministry which we have gleaned from our findings. However, for those new to the use of popular culture in ministry there are some excellent examples of very creative work available in the public domain. For instance, Holy Joes illustrated the use of vocal tracks made meaningful by the context when they played 'The Drugs Don't Work' by The Verve at the sharing of bread and wine during a Greenbelt communion service in 1998, just after the song had reach number one in the singles charts. Jonny Baker created a liturgy around advertising slogans at the biannual conference for the International Association for the Study of Youth Ministry (IASYM) in 2003; the Labyrinth constructed at St Paul's Cathedral in March 2000 combined music, computer technology and traditional iconography to facilitate a personal prayer journey. Many ideas are available on the World Wide Web. We have already mentioned some web sites in the endnotes to the preceding chapters. A web search on 'fresh expressions', 'alternative worship' and 'emerging church' will yield rich rewards. The blogging community also provides link sites and up-to-date ideas and discussions. In particular, we would draw attention to www.Jonnybaker.blogs.com and then suggest that you follow the links to the other blogs from his site. Fuzz Kito in Australia also has a lot to contribute to the debate (www.spirited.net.au/index.php).

For youth work more generally, we found our methodology of presenting extracts of forms of popular culture to groups for discussion provoked interesting and thoughtful conversations. It is a method that could easily be adapted for use in a structured youth work context to explore issues of identity, relationships and spirituality. We hope the principles outlined above will encourage further discussion and stimulate new ideas in the youth work and youth ministry community. We look forward to seeing how things develop.

8

Making disturbing sense of Generation Y

> We argue that the allegedly widespread phenomenon of a
> growth in eclectic spiritual seeking among young people,
> burgeoning on the back of a decline in religion, is illusory.

It is a sobering experience to commission research and then find that it does
not tell you what you had hoped it would! When, as principal of Ridley Hall, I
was involved in commissioning a project which brought together the Theology
Through the Arts programme and our work as trainers for the Centre for Youth
Ministry, I and my colleagues had, I suspect, hoped for confirmation that
young people were open to an overt spiritual search. I think we were also
expecting to find some useful tools for teaching the faith through the popular
arts. What we got was very different, far more revealing, and strategically far
more useful.

This chapter will address the implications of the Generation Y findings for the
Church's future ministry, both with young people and with adults. It will
assess the degree of overt interest in spirituality that the Church can expect
to find in the future.

The second part of the chapter will then use current sociological theory to
account for Generation Y's midi-narrative.

Seeing what we want to see

I am now convinced that there is, in the Church, a tendency to exaggerate the
extent of interest in spirituality in Western culture. I fear that we exaggerate
the significance of those things that we want to see, and downplay evidence
that we do not find so congenial. It is 'a wish fulfilment'.

This tendency is exaggerated further when we have good theological reasons for what we expect to see. Scripture teaches that all human beings are made in God's image. I accept the view that the core meaning of the image of God is that we are made sufficiently like God to be able to have a relationship with him. On this basis all people are made for a relationship with God as their deepest need and primary source of identity. But it is another thing altogether to use this, or other theological convictions, as grounds for accepting congenial evidence and ignoring the less palatable sort.

Debates about secularization theory can also throw us off the track. Just because the more overarching and deterministic theories of secularization are open to substantial question[1] does not in itself provide grounds for accepting that there is a substantial turn back to overt spirituality in the UK.

The New Age

It is, perhaps, the New Age phenomenon which has raised the most hopes among mission-minded Christians. Earlier reactions to the New Age, which saw the whole thing as a demonic conspiracy, have largely been replaced by the belief that, while heterodox, the New Age movement is a 're-enchantment' which represents a turn back to spirituality in the West. Leaving aside the difficulties of definition and the wide range of beliefs and practices involved, the research reported in this book raises some key questions concerning the scale and in particular the longevity of the New Age.

I have no doubts about the significance of the New Age for the mission of the Church. Clearly a section of the adult population has re-engaged with spirituality in recent decades. In a globalized and multicultural society we should not be surprised to find a continuing interest in Eastern faiths and a tendency to gather elements of these eclectically. In the sixties the Boomer generation's highly influential pop culture included an exposure to Eastern and alternative spiritualities from the Beatles down. Pick-and-mix religion does exist, as do a whole variety of spiritual practices. Modernity's loss of innocent trust in scientific progress has spawned a search for alternative, often more holistic, approaches. There is a plethora of therapeutic approaches to the self and its various actual and perceived needs. (Although the therapeutic and the spiritual are certainly not the same thing!)

From one perspective this is substantial. The market share of self-help and mind, body and spirit books is between 7 and 12 per cent and is still growing.[2] The whole area of New Age religion, mind, body and spirit fairs, alternative spiritualities, and so on, is and should be a strategic part of the Church's mission field. The question is whether or not it is a niche within our culture, even if a substantial one, or whether it is evidence of a much more significant overall trend. There has indeed been 'a massive subjective turn . . . a new form of inwardness'[3] in Western culture, but whether or not this is a turn to the overtly spiritual is clearly another matter.

John Drane, perhaps the most adept Christian analyst of (and missioner to) the New Age, identifies 'spiritual seekers' as one of seven categories of people for whom the church should reshape itself and to which it needs to address it mission.[4] The others are 'the desperate poor', 'the hedonists', 'the traditionalists', 'the corporate achievers', 'the secularists' and 'the apathetic'. He does not intend these categories to be totally mutually exclusive, nor to encompass everyone in the population, let alone the majority of young people, and 'one size fits all' will never do as a mission strategy.

A question of scale

One immediate question is that of scale. John Drane claims that the 'spiritual seeker' category is 'probably the most crucial of all, both because of its numerical size, and also because of its influence in the wider culture'. One difficulty here is how to distinguish between actual practitioners and those who hold an eclectic view of spirituality in theory but who do little if anything to act on it. It may be as easy to be a nominal New Ager (without even acknowledging the label) as it is to be a nominal Christian (without knowing much about what the label used to mean). The Kendal Project is a recent study, based on research in the town of Kendal, Cumbria, of the claim 'that traditional forms of religion, particularly Christianity, are giving way to holistic spirituality, sometimes still called New Age'.[5] The study outcomes predict a decline of traditional church attendance down to 3 per cent involved per week, and an increase in involvement in what it calls 'the holistic milieu' to 3 per cent per week. If the New Age niche is below 3 per cent actively participating each week, we do not yet have a spiritual revolution in the UK!

In practice, the significance of the spiritual seekers is almost certainly more substantial than the number of those actively involved. The distinction between being religious and being spiritual has become commonplace and is likely to be latent in the assumed world view of many adults who have no active spiritual or religious involvement. It is perfectly possible that a proportion of these will be awakened to Christian faith by ministries that take it as their starting point. The approaches set out in *Evangelism in a Spiritual*

Age and through a course like Essence,[6] an interactive programme drawing from the teachings of Jesus and the Christian mystics, could be relevant to the substantial number of adults open to or influenced by New Age ideas.

However, the Generation Y research raises a major question about the next generation of adults. Is there any evidence that they will embrace an eclectic approach to spirituality to the same degree as their parents? The Kendal Project makes unproved assumptions. It notes just 1.6 per cent of the population of Kendal and its environs are involved in the holistic milieu (a total of 600 people). Of those, only 1.3 per cent are under 30 years of age. This is infinitesimal, causing me to treat with considerable scepticism the expectation that 'the holistic milieu will attract more participants as they enter their midlives'.[7] This assumes a cultural continuity between the Boomer experience and that of Generation Y which I will challenge later in this chapter, and which is, at least, unproven.

There are legitimate questions about the direction and consequences of cultural change in the UK, but the Generation Y research gives no evidence of a new generation of spiritual seekers. 'Our guess is that young people are echoing broader cultural trends, which the Church cannot ignore' (see Chapter 3).

Vicarious religion

One key question, not considered by the Kendal research, concerns the long-term significance of the large numbers of Britons who claim a religious affiliation in the national census and in similar surveys, without actively belonging to a church.

> The 2001 Census collected information about ethnicity and religious identity. Combining these results shows that while the British population is more culturally diverse than ever before, White Christians remain the largest single group by far. In Great Britain, 40 million people (nearly seven in ten) described their ethnicity as White and their religion as Christian. Majorities of Black people and those from Mixed ethnic backgrounds also identified as Christian (71 and 52 per cent respectively). Only 15 per cent of the British population reported having no religion.[8]

Grace Davie famously described these people as 'believing without belonging',[9] and more recently introduced the notion of 'vicarious religion',[10] meaning 'religion performed by an active minority on behalf of a much larger number'. Believing without belonging involves a level of individual belief without any commitment to a religious institution. Vicarious religion also implies a level of approval of the existence and purpose of religious institutions.

The current cultural climate has seen a new tolerance of (and suspicion of) the role of religious voices in the public square. Religion certainly has a new public face.[11] But this is on the grounds of tolerance and pluralism, which have largely replaced the earlier sacred/secular divide. It has not automatically made religious voices more influential. Religion can still be tolerated as being 'for those who like it', and treated vicariously – 'someone needs to do it'. A leading Salvation Army evangelist remarked that people today 'will trust us with their social problems but not with their souls'. Vicarious religion may well mean that people will trust the Church of England to educate their children in its schools, but not trust it with their spiritual well-being.

Key questions raised by this study are: What happens to the children of these non-affiliated believers? Do they retain the level of belief received from their parents? Will they, as adults, be the generation that neither believes nor belongs, but perhaps approves of vicarious religion? The Generation Y research suggests that this could be the case.

How long?

There is already a range of views about the longevity of the beliefs of those who believe without belonging. It seems clear that those who never engage with worship or with the Church's teaching ministry will often grow more vague in their 'Christian' beliefs. They will continue to understand themselves as Christian and to indicate that fact in national surveys, but their faith may bear minimal resemblance to the Church's historic creeds. This follows Robin Gill's 'cultural theory of church going'.[12]

> Most people born before the Second World War will have been to church and/or Sunday school in their youth, whereas those currently at school will not. In other words, the latter will have little experience of the culture that nurtures Christian beliefs, and are, thus, less likely than an older generation to share them.[13]

In addition, a recent report of the British Household Survey[14] confirms that parents are the most significant influence on children's attitude to religion, but claims that institutional religion has a 'half-life' of one generation: that is, 'two non-religious parents successfully pass on their lack of faith', whereas 'two religious parents have roughly a 50–50 chance of passing on their beliefs'. This research concludes that 'Younger people most often hold their beliefs as part of a view of life which they do not even recognise as spiritual.'[15]

Mission-shaped Church pointed out that 40 per cent of adults in England and Wales are non-churched.[16] They have had no regular involvement with any church either as adults or children. Thus the proportion of young people with any faith background at all is most likely to be in substantial decline. Some strategic approaches to this changing missionary context will be suggested in the next chapter.

The construction of Generation Y's Happy midi-narrative

The findings of the Generation Y research concerning the Happy midi-narrative fit well within a number of emphases in contemporary sociology of culture and sociology of knowledge. Zygmunt Bauman, for example, remarks that, 'The pursuit of happiness and meaningful life has become the major preoccupation of life politics, shifting from the construction of a *better tomorrow* to a *different today.*'[17]

As we have already seen, young people are substantially ignorant of Christian beliefs and values. But this, of itself, does not explain the almost total lack of interest in transformative spirituality found in the Generation Y research. This is best explained once we have grasped that the world view and sense of identity of Generation Y are constructed differently from those of the previous generations.

The American pastoral theologian Tex Sample warns that:

> Our senses, our feelings, our bodies, and our ways of engaging life are culturally and historically structured. We do not have some singular human nature that is the same in all times and places, but rather we are in great part made up of the practices, the relations, the forms of life and the times of which we are a part. I really am 'wired differently' from my children and my grandchildren. What speaks to me does not speak to them.[18]

Sample is not denying that all human beings are made in the image of God and thus have a common core, which unites them as human. He is pointing out the power of culture to shape how we see and live in the world.

Those who live in a different culture or social era from previous generations both see and shape their lives differently from those previous generations. Steven Miles applies this to young people at the start of the twenty-first century.

> Although the ups and downs of social change are experienced through youth lifestyles, the way in which young people engage with these lifestyles is through *the construction of their identities* and the negotiation of the relationship between structure (the external forces of society) and agency (their efforts and actions).[19]

Miles is saying that the study of lifestyle and the construction of identity is the best way to understand young people today, and that it has supplanted earlier approaches, for example subcultural theory.

The generations described in this study have all been living through major social and cultural transition. It is this change which helps to explain the power of Generation Y's midi-narrative and the exclusion of transformative spirituality.

Modernity to postmodernity (or late modernity – or choose your title!)

Contemporary generational theory (Boomers, X and Y) only makes sense when understood within the major cultural shift within Western societies from modernity to post- (or late) modernity. Recent generations have experienced the world differently because the world has changed substantially. During the lifetime of these three generations our culture has gone through a transition from an era primarily formed from the eighteenth-century Enlightenment, into a new era, which we have not been able to name until recently – hence, the proliferation of the use of the term 'postmodern'. To quote Walter Truett Anderson, 'We are charging headlong into a new era ... The word commonly used to describe this era is "postmodern." ... Postmodern is a makeshift word we use until we have decided what to name the baby.'[20]

David Lyon describes it in this way:

> Postmodernity is a kind of interim situation where some characteristics of modernity have been inflated to such an extent that modernity becomes scarcely recognizable as such, but exactly what the new situation is – or even whether any new situation can become 'settled' is unclear.[21]

I do not wish to get involved in the academic arguments about the degree of continuity between the 'modern' and the 'postmodern'. Although I believe it is time to finish with the 'postmodern' vocabulary.[22] 'Post' implies that we are still in a period of transition, waiting for a new era to take shape. To some extent this is true. As Zygmunt Bauman has said, 'We have not been here before, so we do not know what to expect.'[23] But, in practice, we have been here for some time now. The basic shape and central values of our culture are clearly in place. Whatever the debate about 'postmodernism' the shape of 'postmodernity' (or 'the new modernity' or 'high modernity' or 'liquid modernity') is generally agreed. Only the title is in question. Much more importantly for our study, this is the only culture Generation Y has ever known! Language of cultural change is alien to them, apart from references to the speed of technological change. Inevitably they have no experience of the era that came before they were born. They really are 'wired differently'.

The three key coordinates of Generation Y's culture

David Lyon helpfully outlines the key cultural ingredients that shape Generation Y.

> The inflated characteristics of modernity, which give rise to postmodern premonitions, relate above all to communication and information technologies and to the tilt towards consumerism. Both are bound up with the restructuring of capitalism that has been under way since at least the last quarter of the twentieth century.[24]

In other words, three major transitions interlock and radically change the way we experience and interpret the world. They are the shifts from producer to consumer, from industrial to electronic society and from sovereign nation states to a globalized world. I will address each in turn, but it is the integration of the three that gives them their profound impact.

Consumerism

We have moved from a society which shaped its members primarily as producers – those who believed in progress, in producing something that contributed to the better life that was certain to come through education and hard work – to a society which shapes its members first and foremost by its need for them to play the role of consumer. As Bauman expresses it:

> The difference is one of emphasis, but that shift does make an enormous difference to virtually every aspect of society, culture and individual life. The differences are so deep and ubiquitous that they fully justify speaking of our society as a separate and distinct kind – a consumer society.[25]

In this sense, Generation Y is the first 100 per cent consumer generation.

Lyon explains:

> Where once Westerners might have found their identity, their social togetherness and the ongoing life of their society in the area of production, these are today increasingly found through consumption. Its not that companies are producing less, or that people no longer work. Rather the meaning of these activities has altered. We are what we buy. We relate to others who consume the same way that we do. And the overarching system of capitalism is fuelled by, and geared to stimulating, consumption.[26]

The central value of such a society has moved from progress to choice: the absolute right of freedom to choose. 'Choice lies at the centre of consumerism, both as its emblem and as its core value.'[27]

It is worth noting that Grace Davie describes the central shift of attitude towards religion as from 'religion as a form of obligation to an increasing emphasis on consumption'.[28] There is, she says,

> An additional and overriding mutation that is taking place in this part of the world both within and outside the historic churches, that is from forms of religion that are imposed or inherited to forms of religion that are primarily chosen.[29]

As we have already indicated, 'Belief in God is an optional matter, a consumer choice.'

In this society everyone becomes a consumer.

> The amount of money available to individuals for consumption varies enormously, but virtually everyone today is a consumer to some degree. The poor have fewer resources than the rich, most

ethnic and racial minority groups have much less to spend than members of the majority, children fewer means than adults, and so on, but all are enmeshed in the consumer culture. Even those who live on the streets survive off the discards and charity of that wildly affluent culture.[30]

Furthermore, everything becomes a consumer choice.

Areas of social life that were previously free of the demands of the market place, including religion, have had to adapt to a world where the needs and demands of the consumer are apparently paramount ... Consumerism is arguably *the* religion of the late twentieth [now early twenty-first] century.[31]

At its worst this can create a very self-indulgent society.

Pleasure lies at the heart of consumerism. It finds in consumerism a unique champion which promises to liberate it both from its bondage to sin, duty and morality as well as its ties to faith, spirituality and redemption. Consumerism proclaims pleasure not merely as the right of every individual but also as every individual's obligation to him or her self ... The pursuit of pleasure, untarnished by guilt or shame, becomes the new image of the good life.[32]

This is not far from the vision of the 'happy life' that emerged in this study.

It would be as unfair to treat all youth culture as hedonistic, as it would to treat the whole adult population under Drane's 'hedonist' category. Young people are not more selfish than previous generations, far from it, but these cultural developments have a long history.[33] Generation Y is the heir to a cultural process lasting many decades. In the Generation Y research there was a 'deep tension' within the young people's attitude to consumer culture, but that culture was also the amniotic fluid in which they lived. This is not a generation that has the option of living outside of consumerism, as long as it chooses to live in the West. Part of the Church's mission will be to help this generation to critique it from within.

Consumerism also provides the perspective for evaluating truth claims. The language of shopping provides the vocabulary for assessing truth.

When many voices can be heard, who can say that one should be heeded more than another? ... When the only criteria left for choosing between them are learned in the marketplace, then truth appears as a commodity. We hear the people 'buy into' a belief or that, rather than rejecting a dogma as false, they 'cannot buy' this or that viewpoint.[34]

If the majority of young people have little or no accurate knowledge of the Christian story it is not likely to be something they buy into. Nor are they likely to make shopping expeditions to the specialist outlets where it could be found!

Electronic media

The growth of communication and information technologies is one of the most striking and transformative changes of the twentieth century. They do not in themselves transform anything, but they contribute to the establishment of novel contexts of social interaction ... They help to alter the significance of face-to-face relationships while simultaneously bringing all of us into daily contact with cultures once remote or strange.[35]

The impact of electronic media has been immense. It is not only relationships that have been impacted. Understandings of truth have also been changed. Few Western people can escape the reality of our pluralist world. 'There has been one fundamental reason for the increasing pluralism of our era: it has been united by current technologies into an instantaneous 24-hour information world.'[36] Indeed the endless supply of messages can make relativism seem self-evident, and consumer choice the only way to pick and mix a world view. 'The sheer overload of broadcast imagery and sounds confronts the consumer with a total collage environment.'[37] To many people today, all truths are relative except the truth that all truths are relative!

It once seemed easy enough to distinguish between truth and falsity, objectivity and subjectivity, good reasons and bad, and even morality and immorality. Yet, those days have largely vanished, as television, radio, books, newspapers, e-mail and passing acquaintances inundate us with differences in perspective, values, and understandings. In what particular words can we place our trust when confronted with infinite variations in the real and the good?[38]

It is important to note that this is not the inevitable meaning of electronic media, just their dominant impact at this stage of history. However, any form of exclusive truth claim will seem alien in a world of multiple messages. The developed skill with which a young person will choose which emails and texts to respond to and which are 'spam' can quickly filter out the claims of both religion and spiritualities.

Other writers point out that we have entered a 'second orality' – a move from book culture to screen culture. This move has caused significant changes in the way people learn, changes which the Church has not always adapted to well. Adults who were shaped by a limited-choice, terrestrial TV culture, are raising children shaped by a digital and interactive one.

> TV is controlled by adults. Kids are passive observers. In contrast, children control much of their world on the Net. It is something they do themselves; they are users and they are active. They do not just observe, they participate. This makes the Internet fundamentally different from previous communications innovations, such as the development of the printing press or the introduction of radio and television broadcasting.[39]

Sherry Turkle (Professor of the Sociology of Science at MIT) writes that 'A nascent culture of simulation is affecting our ideas about mind, body, self and machine . . . in much of this it is our children who are leading the way, and adults who are anxiously trailing behind.'[40] Young people are at ease with communications technologies. 'Children and young people are in the "avant garde" of many contemporary developments in the electronic media.'[41] Which of us has not asked our children to show us how to use our computers? Generation Y has grown up in a culture of digital interactive communication. This has a profound impact on how community is understood. In one sense it is highly individualistic. 'Twentieth century communications have made possible an increasing proportion of remote relationships.'[42]

> Instead of sharing in community we now prefer to face not other people but the monitor, logging into a cyber-personal internet which grants us hitherto unimaginable access to a vast electronic cosmos, but which simultaneously divorces us from flesh and blood reality itself.[43]

Television programming is now based on a narrow cast rather than broadcast basis, because the assumption is that the generations will rarely watch programmes together, because most, if not all, family members will have their own television. The Walkman and the iPod also provide distinctly individual pleasures.

And yet there is an instinctive community between those who use them. The growing phenomenon of young people having their own web page illustrates this search for community. 'Publishing on the Web for young people is motivated by the desire to participate in, or create, some kind of "community" ... Publishing here is an attempt to speak directly *with* rather than *to* the audience.'[44] So personal web sites are an expression of the need of community. Such web sites, combined with young people's dexterity on MSN, means that the distinction between the written and the oral blurs. 'Speaking online takes a written form and writing in cyberspace almost has an oral function.'[45] The mobile phone, and young people's dexterity at texting contribute to the same phenomenon.

This research has examined young people's use of narrative and story in some depth. I simply note that the emphasis on narrative fits well into an age of visual digital media. The contrast is not between electronic media and storytelling, but between both of these and any assumption that Christian, or any other communication, needs to involve the sequential presentation of concepts or doctrines, if it is to be objective. It is abstract, one-way 'communication' that fails to communicate to Generation Y.

The apparently limitless supply of electronic imagery and information does give a degree of plausibility to Generation Y's belief that its midi-narrative is all that is necessary. 'With their markets and media, modern societies have developed what amount to substitute forms that seem to render superfluous any action of God's Spirit.'[46] To quote Tex Sample again,

> It is no secret that those most influenced by electronic culture participate in church at far lower levels than those of previous generations. I believe that the failure of the church, as of yet, to deal with the changes brought on by an electronic culture is a basic factor in the lower levels of participation of post-World War 2 electronic generations.[47]

Andrew Walker states, 'We have a story but no one can see it. We tell the story but no one can hear it. We have a fundamental problem of communication because *we are still bound to an anachronistic literary culture.*'[48]

Manuel Castells has charted the development of the 'network society' in which flows of information advertisements, capital and power are more influential than geographical spaces.[49] Overall, 'what is at stake in these technical innovations is . . . a broad and extensive change in the culture'.[50] But this changed culture is Generation Y's natural home. According to Castells, this is not merely a change in emphasis but 'The emergence of a new social structure'[51] – but it is not 'new' to Generation Y.

By definition, these media are global in scope. They contribute to globalization and carry the messages of a global consumer society. The third coordinate of Generation Y's culture is globalization.

Globalization, time and space

'Globalization as a concept refers to both the compression of the world and the intensification of consciousness of the world as a whole.'[52] In other words, the process of globalization also changes the way we experience and see the world.

In his Reith lectures Anthony Giddens stated: 'Globalisation is restructuring the ways in which we live, and in a very profound manner . . . Globalisation also influences everyday life as much as it does events happening on a world scale.'[53] Globalization would have no great impact upon us if it did not make things different locally. 'The key to its cultural impact is in the transformation of localities themselves.'[54]

In practice, the three coordinates, consumerism, electronic media and globalization, combine. The media open up a wide range of consumer lifestyle choices from all over the globe, and those who have the resources exercise their right to choose and network with those with whom they find interests in common, often creating a community of common interest more on a network than a neighbourhood basis. A globalized world is experienced and seen differently from its predecessor.

The other dimension of globalization relevant to our study is that it creates a changed experience of space and time, which are core matrices of the development of identity.

David Lyon writes, 'at a profound social level, time and space, the very matrix of human social life, are undergoing radical social restructuring'.[55] According to Paul Virilio, we are at 'The end of the era of space and the emergence of the era of speed.'[56] This cultural shift also involves a change of emphasis from the future to the present. Neither modernity nor postmodernity has much 'time' for the past. For moderns it was simply the marker to measure the great progress which had been made. For postmoderns it is a source of stories and symbols to cannibalize or rewrite. But postmodernity has rejected modernity's ideological belief in progress and a better future, and refocused on the present as the one thing to be sure of.

Zygmunt Bauman illustrates this well by contrasting the savings book with the credit card. 'Modernity extolled the delay of gratification ... the postmodern world ... preaches delay of payment. If the savings book was the epitome of modern life, the credit card is the paradigm of the postmodern one.'[57] But the experience of the present is also changing. 'Slow, steady, sequential time is being displaced by the instant and the simultaneous, and fixed space gives way to flows – of information, of capital, of power.'[58] For many people today, 'the future is little more than an extended present'.[59]

If this fairly represents the world view of Generation Y, then it gives another reason for the absence of transformative spirituality. Most religious traditions, especially the Christian one, have a vision of a shared future to work towards, and a sense of the obstacles to be overcome if we are to reach that future. This research indicates that Generation Y tends to work with a much shorter view, for the central concerns of religion and spirituality are beyond its horizons.

X and Y

Generation X is the generation for whom modernity has failed to deliver its dream of progress. There have been a number of excellent studies on this generation,[60] but I wish to make just one point. It is a hinge generation, raised in modernity but living in 'postmodernity'. It is a generation of people with two cultures fighting inside them. They have much to teach us, and need particular mission strategies, but *they are not the shape of the future*. That rests with Generation Y.

Furlong and Cartmel's study of young people's experience claims that 'Young people today are growing up in a different world to that experienced by previous generations', because they are 'subject to uncertainties which were not part of day to day life for previous generations'.[61] Generation Y represents the first fully formed generation of a new era. There will, of course, be generations to follow. There will still be rapid change. Some form of generation gap will always be with us. But my argument is that this generation represents the first glimpse of an era to come, which may well last many generations. The significance of the Generation Y research is the glimpse it may give us of adult generations to come.

Culture as a blindfold

A world view can act both as a lens through which to see the world and as a blindfold which prevents us from seeing it fully. Generation Y's midi-narrative clearly functions in both ways. St Paul describes this negative dimension as 'the god of this world blinding minds' (2 Corinthians 4.4). By 'this world' he means the whole construct of a culture and its underlying values, which can blind people about their true situation and their need of Christ.

I have already suggested that this blindfold is constructed from the interaction of a consumerist mindset, and a globalized and electronically connected world. One other dimension can be added to complete the recipe. I have already referred to the subjective or inwards turn Western culture has made.[62] How, as individuals, we *feel* about anything becomes increasingly important and the basis of our authenticity. (Being authentic seems to be an important Generation Y value.) To a far greater degree than in previous eras Western culture in general, and Generation Y in particular, looks inwards for the final source of authority. This is clearly an aspect of the trend towards individualism in Western societies. According to Ulrich Beck, 'Individualization is becoming the social structure of the second modernity itself.'[63] 'History shrinks to the (eternal) present, and everything revolves around the axis of one's personal ego and personal life.'[64]

This fits with recent studies in the decline of social capital over recent decades.[65] It does not contradict the findings of this research that the essence of the deep end of the Happy midi-narrative 'is more relational than individualistic' (Chapter 3 above). Young people clearly seek happiness through relationships. Rather it refers to the collapse of larger political and philosophical visions in wider society. According to Beck the consequence is that 'We are all asked to seek biographical solutions to systemic contradictions',[66] to find a personal lifestyle that resolves the ambiguities inherent in our society. If anything, this makes personal friendships even more important and places a pressure on them which it is sometimes beyond their capacity to bear.

Constructivism: the key to Generation Y's self-understanding

At the heart of Generation Y's world view lies a form of constructivism. Human identity and understandings of truth are not given or revealed but socially constructed. In practice, in everyday life, this is largely assumed as 'common sense'. It is argued *from* rather than argued to. (It is characteristic that just as native speakers of a language are often ignorant of its formal grammar, so those operating from a world view, often do so without consciously reflecting on or invoking the world view.)

If the ideological opponent of the Church in an earlier stage of modernity was secularism, constructivism fills that role today. And like all effective heresies it is partly right. Humans are made in God's image to be culture builders and their sense of identity is built up in that activity. But if the assumption of God is withdrawn from the equation, human beings see themselves as self-generating, entirely within the social and economic constraints of their particular context. When Christians engage with this culture they immediately turn to issues of truth. Most of the secular writing, on the other hand, engages the issue of human identity.

In a consumer culture, identity is constructed through 'lifestyle', that is consumer, choices.

'Lifestyle choice is increasingly important in the constitution of self-identity and daily activity.'[67] David Lyon writes,

> Image and style are now central to identity. Nike running shoes, Levi jeans, Coca-Cola – these and more – all help to give shape to who we are. This is different from binding our identity to work or employment ... and it raises shopping skills to the level of virtue. Likewise our social circle, our peer group, is likely to share consuming patterns in common, more than anything else.[68]

Anthony Giddens, who does not agree with the label 'postmodern' acknowledges that this is a 'novel phenomenon'.[69]

There is a taken-for-granted theology underlying this way of life.

> Identities are constructed through consuming. Forget the idea that who we are is given by God or achieved through hard work in a calling or a career: we shape our malleable image by what we buy – our clothing, our kitchens, and our cars tell the story of who we are (becoming).[70]

Identity is not given through family, let alone the image of God.[71] It may well be that Generation Y has such a benign and idealistic view of family because consumer culture, and its presuppositions, are the shared environment of the whole family. The whole family sings from the same consumerist hymn sheet. A constructivist approach assumes that 'the self has no centre'[72] and that the aesthetic life is the ethically good life and that there is no human nature or true self, with the goal of life an endless pursuit of new experiences, values and vocabularies. Humans are assumed to be self-generating. 'A notion is presented . . . that self-creation is an endless possibility'.[73]

This means that the sharing of the gospel in such a context will involve 'the stumbling block of creation', of our accountability to the creator, long before it reaches the stumbling block of the cross. As one theologian warns us,

> It is the distinction of the human creature, created in the image of God, to be called to exercise its created destiny in *finite* freedom . . . Where it interprets itself as absolute self-created freedom and denies its character as gift, it falls into a bondage from which it can find no escape.[74]

This view of life is given support and plausibility by computer culture.

> A nascent culture of simulation is affecting our ideas about mind, body, self and machine . . . in much of this it is our children who are leading the way, and adults who are anxiously trailing behind. In the story of constructing identity in the culture of simulation, experiences on the Internet figure prominently, but these experiences can only be understood within a larger cultural context. That context is the story of the eroding boundaries between the real and the virtual, the animate and the inanimate, the unitary and the multiple self, which is occurring *both* in fields of advanced scientific research *and* in the patterns of everyday life.[75]

> That such a variety of selves may be available in a range of combinations today is not in itself surprising. They reflect a cultural variety enabled and encouraged above all by new media and globalization. And the way they are constructed relates increasingly to consumer choices, whether playful or serious.[76]

At the heart of postmodernity, and therefore at the heart of Generation Y, is a profound ambiguity about the self. The self must be solid enough to feel like 'me', but flexible enough to keep changing in new circumstances.[77] 'The self is both central and fragmented.'[78] It is created by consumer choice, but who is the self who chooses? Zygmunt Bauman perceptively pointed out that postmodernity is not so much marked by the construction of identity as by the evasion of answerability. 'The hub of postmodern life strategy is not identity building but avoidance of fixation.' 'Keep the options open.'[79]

It should not, then, surprise us that the postmodern understanding of truth is also constructivist. Again the nomadic theme appears. 'We all become nomads, migrating across a system that is too vast to be our own, but in which we are fully involved, translating and transforming bits and elements into local instances of sense.'[80] For Generation X this is a traumatic experience, but for many of Generation Y it is normal and provides a buzz. Bauman's recognition that 'An ever growing number of postmodern men and women ... find the open-endedness of their situation attractive enough to outweigh the anguish of uncertainty' now feels a little dated.

This research emphasizes the danger of imposing the cultural assumptions of a previous era upon Generation Y and emphasizes the danger of treating the uncertainty of life as a problem when it is freely embraced. Generation Y also rejects the victim status that characterized Generation X.

Chapter 7 has emphasized the inappropriateness of 'deficit models' for mission among Generation Y. It may be easy to see the 'deficits' of the midi-narrative and to identify negative trends and individual victims, but most within Generation Y are perfectly happy in it. When life does not work out as happily as their aspirations, they do not necessarily question their world view. Generation Y's Happy midi-narrative makes perfect sense within the shape and values of contemporary Western society. It is not the world view of all young people. But it is for many. It is already the world view of an increasing number of adults, and indicates the shape of things to come. It is likely to provide the Church with the greatest long-term missionary challenge.

This is not a case of projecting adolescent attitudes into adulthood. Although there is a strong argument that consumer culture retains many adolescent features![81] Nor is it simply a matter of ages and stages of faith, although that approach (of which, in its popularized form, I am very sceptical) also allows for adults to be stuck at a particular stage of development. Rather, it is the sociology that convinces me. Recent sociological studies of youth culture demonstrate the ways in which it is shaped by the overall culture.[82] This is not surprising. Young people live and form their identities in a world shaped and run by adults.

Of course, some young people and some adults will be disillusioned when life does not deliver the promised happiness, but this does not guarantee that they will change their world view. Some may well begin to search for God, but it is as likely that they will simply become fatalistic, or conclude that they themselves are to blame for failing to make the right lifestyle choices.

A change in world view and lifestyle only takes place when the plausibility of the current world view and lifestyle is undermined by experience *and* a genuinely plausible alternative is visible. To give Tex Sample the final word:

> Much of electronic culture is based in a consumerist story that has crept into a host of the forms of life at work in the wider society and in the church. This is a profoundly distorted story. It will require alternative, oppositional, and subversive resistance. But such resistance cannot be simply based on a negative of opposition. The resistance will need a story of its own, one more powerful than the consumerist.[83]

Just how the Church might address this challenge will be the subject of the final chapter.

9

Reconnecting with Generation Y – and all those like them

Mismatch

The large mismatch between the Church's world view and young people's Happy midi-narrative has some major implications for the future shape of the Church's mission. Although there is an inevitable adolescent element to the attitudes we have examined, I have tried to demonstrate that they are coherent with the substantial cultural changes that are impacting Western societies. It is much more likely that youth cultures are now changing because the overall culture is changing, than that youth cultures change in isolation from, or in reaction against, the overall culture.[1] In other words, we cannot console ourselves with the suggestion that they will simply grow out of it!

Mission-shaped Church draws urgent attention to the growing cultural gap between world and church. It identifies 40 per cent of adults as non-churched, those who have never had any form of church connection. In addition, there is the much larger percentage of young people with a similar lack of experience, or knowledge of the Christian faith.[2] It is highly likely that the attitudes identified in this research will represent the view of an increasing proportion of these. If we are to take this seriously some strategic planning will be necessary. My aim in this final chapter is to suggest some component parts for that planning.

Overall we are faced with the task of reconnecting our church to our culture. Regarding some, those called the de-churched in *Mission-shaped Church*,[3] this is a task of connecting back to people we have lost. This is a major ministry and will need a substantial investment of energy. But the primary task for the long term will have to be connecting with the non-churched, who will soon include the majority of the children of the de-churched, and already include the majority of Generation Y. In their case we are not reconnecting with them individually, because they have never been connected, but we are seeking to reconnect them as a generation to the Christian gospel, as previous generations have known it.

Don't panic

The first reaction should be to avoid panic. In each new cultural era, or cross-cultural venture through the centuries, the Church has been faced with a world view and way of life that had previously managed perfectly well without the gospel. In each context the Church has learned how to engage with its new cultural setting, following the guidance of the Holy Spirit. Throughout church history this has been done well and it has been done badly. When done badly it has tended to leave future generations with baggage they could well have done without. But the missionary story also contains many examples of good practice. Some cultures may prove harder for the Church to connect with than others, but none are harder for the Holy Spirit. There is no effective alternative to inculturation, to engaging people with the gospel within and as appropriate to their own culture and world view.

The Church's everyday mission should not be grinding to a halt. The regular work of personal witness, of Alpha and Emmaus courses, of baptisms, weddings and funerals, mums and tots groups, youth work, seeker services, and the like, needs to continue. There is no new strategy needed to replace mission-minded churches, which are deeply engaged with their communities and hospitable to newcomers. In one sense we just need more of them! The same applies to youth ministries.

In recent years there has been a revolution in youth ministry which has seen older organizations, like Crusaders and Youth for Christ, reinvent themselves, and new groups like Soul Survivor and the Message Trust come into being. The standard of Christian youth ministry has been raised through the training of scores of professionally qualified workers; and a new set of values for relational youth ministry, which empowers young people to take responsibility for their own ministry and mission, has been put into place. This is a substantial investment for the task that now faces us. But these resources must be released to engage with the mission field as it is, and not trapped by the churches' insistence on recycling old and outdated models of mission.

Mission-shaped Church argues that 40 per cent of the adult population are still within reach of familiar models of Christian mission. This is no time to stop, just because we have questions about what will prove appropriate in the future. However, it is time to reflect, because a clear time limit may be being set for stand-alone evangelistic programmes, based on a 'come to us' strategy. These still make up far too large a proportion of our evangelistic activities. As one youth worker told me, 'I know how to lead young people to Jesus. What I don't know is how to meet my pastor's expectations at the same time.'

There is a wonderful simplicity at the heart of the gospel, which ensures that neither status nor a special level of intellectual capacity is required for reconciliation with God. At the same time the impact of the gospel is so wonderfully diverse that there are many bridges to Christ. Our culture requires a diverse strategy. One size cannot fit all. John Drane's seven categories,[4] mentioned in the last chapter, provide a good theoretical starting point for planning. But there is no effective alternative to local research and a local mission audit.

Patient sowing

We have argued that 'the Christian faith often has little relevance simply because it is largely unknown' (Chapter 7). Contemporary strategies for evangelism, which use a catechumenate or process approach, already start further back than was the case a few decades ago, because they assume less knowledge of the faith. The level of ignorance of the Christian faith among Generation Y warns us that in the coming decades we will have to patiently sow the gospel story into our culture assuming no prior knowledge. Where the gospel story is not known, we need to tell it. If this is not done, as a consistent long-term strategy, the supply of people for other, more directly evangelistic ministries will run dry. It is difficult for many older churchgoers to imagine the current degree of biblically illiteracy in our culture. But the attitude that they 'ought' to know the Christian story will not help. We need to tell them, but in an appropriate way. Our research shows that the story needs to be told in a way that allows the audience some responsibility to work out the meaning for themselves. Telling Generation Y what to believe will not work. Telling the Christian story, in a way that raises questions about their own stories, will be an important skill. Jesus use of parables provides an important model, as does his patience with the disciples, when they were slow to understand. Through this patience, the disciples grew to a point where they were capable of grasping the truth at a more profound level. At the root of his patience, and ours, lies the conviction that the Father was at work in this process, revealing Jesus' true identity (Matthew 11.25; 16.15–16).

The sowing metaphor is important. It reminds us, from our experience of nature, that long-term patient work is worth the effort. Sowers do not see immediate results. Nor are they the source of any resultant growth, which follows in its own time. But if they had not sowed the seed, the growth could not have occurred. The biblical material about the sowing of the gospel is well known. It implies that, like a seed, the gospel has a life of its own, and that God gives the growth. It is time to emphasize both the patience and the faith of the sower. Recent generations of missionary endeavour have relied upon the impact of the gospel in still earlier generations, much more than we have acknowledged. But that 'gospel capital' is now used up. We can no longer presume on our culture to bear the gospel story from generation to generation on our behalf. We have to commit ourselves to sowing in each generation, as much for the sake of the next, as for a more immediate harvest. The gospel story has great power and it will attract some people as they hear it properly for the first time. But this must not distract us from the long-term task of sowing.

Reconnecting

Because post-Christendom is not the same as pre-Christendom, this work of sowing will often involve reconnecting our culture to its own heritage. Centuries of Christian influence have left evidence of Christian believing all over British society. Reconnecting people to this is not straightforward, as the consumerist, pick-and-mix approach of the Happy midi-narrative often disconnects Christian symbols from the Christian story. The classic example is the singer Madonna wearing a crucifix as a fashion item. Our attempts will require a degree of sophistication. Remembering the Generation Y researchers' unsuccessful use of a Salvador Dali crucifixion image when trial-running the project, I am not suggesting using art as propaganda, or as a quick way to tell the Christian story and get a response. But education is inseparably connected to a history in which religion played a central part, and our culture is saturated in visual imagery. This can provide us with many storytelling opportunities, and occasions when, starting with an image, we can say 'this is that'. For example, the Images of Salvation resource connects mediaeval religious imagery to the biblical themes and stories it portrays. We need to develop these reconnecting skills, and take full advantage of the range of Christian research projects, which work in this area.[5]

The Church has a huge and obvious resource for this – our historic buildings. The national census reported that 80 per cent of Britons visit a church building at least once per year, most of them for the heritage rather than for worship. The days when it could be assumed that most people know why many churches are built in the shape of a cross, or have a tower or spire, or what the stories in the windows are, are fading. But the heritage industry is growing. We will need to develop training courses on how to teach the faith through interpreting a building. Many churches provide leaflets and displays to explain the architecture and the historical features of their buildings. Few seem to have integrated the teaching of the faith, rather than local history, into the process. Cathedrals have a major strategic opportunity for this, but the same applies to any historic church building. Stained glass was used to teach biblical stories to an illiterate majority. We need to learn to use it to teach a biblically illiterate majority. In our culture pilgrims have turned into tourists. The many tourists who visit our ancient churches may be helped on the first steps to becoming pilgrims again.

Another obvious opportunity for reconnecting is provided by church schools. These have the unique opportunity of being both distinctively Christian, while being properly inclusive in their admissions policies. A church school is founded on Christian values, while being properly respectful about other faiths in a multicultural society and giving them their appropriate place in the curriculum. But it is most certainly the place where large numbers of children can become familiar with the biblical story and its relevance. This is by no means automatic, nor easy. But it is critical.

Our civic life provides another opportunity. Anglican clergy officiate at many civic occasions. Vicarious religion,[6] where the majority expect the Church to act on their behalf, without their own active participation, creates congregations at a wide number of civic occasions, or in response to tragedies. These used to be occasions where clergy would speak from and apply some aspect of the Christian story which was common knowledge in the culture. Increasingly we will have to tell the story before we apply it.

None of this is intended to be about direct evangelism. It is about the intentional, sensitive, but unapologetic, long-term sowing of the biblical story back into our culture.

The sowing of the Christian story sounds innocent and ineffectual, but it has the power to be profoundly subversive. The Christian story, once understood, subverts other, lesser stories – including the Happy midi-narrative! We will return to the theme of subversion later in the chapter.

Incarnational church planting

A church which has lost touch with large parts of its culture, needs to develop ways to relocate itself. The emphasis in *Mission-shaped Church* on 'fresh expressions of church' is designed to affirm a whole range of pioneering projects, but also to encourage a wide range of new initiatives. (This is within a clear commitment to a 'mixed economy' church, where mission-shaped traditional parishes and fresh expressions of church are interdependent.) Within this strategy of interdependence new initiatives will increasingly be made on a generational or network basis, rather than a territorial one.

The perspective Andrew Walls has given on the international missionary movement has equal force at home.

> The territorial 'from-to' idea that underlay the older missionary movement has to give way to a concept much more like that of Christians within the Roman Empire in the second and third centuries: parallel presences in different circles and at different levels, each seeking to penetrate within and beyond its circle. This does not prevent movement and interchange and enterprise ... but it forces revision of concepts, images, attitudes, and methods that arose from the presence of a Christendom that no longer exists.[7]

In my view the most important insight of *Mission-shaped Church* concerned inculturation.[8] This is an incarnational approach, which at its heart involves meeting people where they are and serving them in ways they find beneficial. It aspires to establish good mutual relationships in which the missioners receive as much as give. It allows the gospel to be shared, and the gospel community to take shape, as the Holy Spirit leads. These are essential skills for anyone willing to make a long-term commitment to embodying the gospel among the non-churched. A theological principle is at stake.

> The issue is not relevance as far as the Church is concerned. The issue is Incarnation. When so called 'traditional' churches are out of touch with the people who live around them, the problem is not that they are irrelevant, but that they are not incarnational.[9]

The effectiveness of our mission in the coming generations may well depend on the capacity of individual Christians, projects and congregations to embody the gospel in a changing culture. This has always been largely the case, but for many centuries there was also the resource of an inherited body of Christian knowledge in our culture.

Prior mission

In Chapter 7 we proposed the development of 'prior mission' as the starting point for the Church's mission with Generation Y. The work of Ann Morisy[10] and others shows that this is already necessary with many adults, and increasingly will be so for Generation Y. Prior mission is not pre-evangelism rebranded. Pre-evangelism is an exercise in apologetics. It assumes a degree of knowledge of the Christian faith and seeks to establish the relevance of that faith, and to remove intellectual objections to belief. Prior mission is about appropriate contact and an appropriate starting point with those who have little or no knowledge of the faith, little interest in it, and who are content not only with the content of their view of life, but with its horizons as well.

This sort of mission will involve meeting people where they are and seeking to establish the maximum common ground. It will involve positive action to benefit them, regardless of their immediate responsiveness to the Christian message or otherwise.

Ann Morisy speaks of mission in the 'foundational domain'. She writes, 'the aim of our work in the foundational domain is to help people embrace the possibility of God'.[11] Since 'without faith it is impossible to please God, for whoever would approach him must believe that he exists and that he rewards those who seek him' (Hebrews 11.6), this really is foundational. Morisy sees this ministry as one that awakens the imagination. 'This means awakening within people the capacity to be astonished and to be surprised by the *more* in life.'[12]

There is nothing new in Christian mission addressing people's capacity to understand, before it shares the joys and demands of the gospel. Workers among tribal peoples will find ways to learn a new language, write it down, teach the people to read, and work on sensitive translations of the Bible, as part of the long evangelistic process. Best practice would see all of this as for the well-being of the people concerned, rather than merely being instrumental for evangelism.

Chapter 7 indicated that this will involve starting where young people are, rather than where we would like them to be, and helping them to articulate their own questions, rather than expecting them to respond to ours. In particular it will focus on character and the formation of identity, and help young people to identify 'the person they want to become'. The same applies to many adults. The consumer world view described in the previous chapter prioritizes and problematizes questions of identity and identity formation.

Traditionally, Christian mission has started with the proclamation of doctrine and concluded with ethics. As best practice this was open about the cost of discipleship: 'If you are going to be a Christian this is how you are expected to live.' At its worst it became, 'Although we didn't tell you, this is how you are now expected to live.' Mission to Generation Y is likely to start with ethics, not as an authoritative demand for observation of the whole Christian ethical code, but with the teaching of Jesus in particular, and the Christian moral tradition as a whole, offered initially as a resource for coping with life.[13] The television series *No Sex Please, We're Teenagers*, shown on BBC2 in autumn 2005, provided a fascinating example.

Our multi-choice consumer society has made lifestyle magazines and lifestyle guidance into a growth industry. 'What do I choose?' quickly raises the question 'How do I choose?' 'How do I choose?' raises the question 'What sort of person do I want to be?' 'The ultimate question at the heart of choosing is not what we wish to acquire, but what kind of world we are seeking to be a part of.'[14] These are not merely adolescent questions, but pervade our individualized society. The willingness to walk alongside our fellow human beings as they explore, or are encouraged to explore, questions of identity, is an essential form of prior mission in the foundational domain. This is not a 'deficit' approach, but one which enables people to make their own discovery that 'there is more'. It fits the 'narrative development' approach recommended earlier in this book.

Clearly Generation Y's world view assumes a form of self-actualizing. It has implicitly placed the self at the heart of the person, in the place of God, and ultimately must be challenged if the gospel is to be presented faithfully. But the question 'what sort of person do I want to be?' raises questions of purpose and identity which are essentially theological. If, at a later stage, people are to recognize their sin, that they have fallen short of the glory of God, one step along the way is to recognize that they are falling short of their ideal self, of what they could, even 'ought' to be.

The issue of character also raises a further question about how character is formed. Some dimensions of contemporary society actually corrode character. 'How can I be the sort of person I want to be?' is a real and challenging question, however narrow a person's horizons. The Christian tradition directly links the formation of character to spirituality and worship. Character questions form an identifiable bridge between formative and transformative spirituality.

Pastoral ministry: Attending to the deficit of the Happy midi-narrative

Our research has identified a tension between young people's actual world and their ideal one. Once again the same applies to many adults. Those who believe they have a right to be happy will often struggle in the real world, even in affluent societies. Generation Y's general view that life is benign contrasts strangely with the increasing figures concerning eating disorders, substance abuse, teenage suicide attempts, bullying, sexual abuse and the like.[15] There are clearly winners and losers around the Happy midi-narrative.

The levels of trust in family that we discovered were encouraging. The 'generation gap', as described in previous youth work theory, no longer exists in the same way. However, in some cases this was more an expression of what 'ought to be' than what was actually the case.

Many young people and adults need a safe space when they are in pain. Pain about profoundly broken family relationships is not naturally expressed in public groups talking to a researcher. The experience of the welfare team at Soul Survivor events is that there is a surprisingly deep pool of unaddressed pastoral need, even in a largely middle-class gathering of teenagers. Whatever a person's knowledge or view of God, they need love, help and support when they are in distress. The Church has deep resources for pastoral care that will remain at a premium. It is not enough to do our mission through our pastoral care, but it is still essential.

Subversion

Ultimately the Happy midi-narrative has to be challenged. It is a fraud. It is a midi-narrative trying to fulfil the role of a meta-narrative. It needs subverting, and it cannot be morally responsible simply to wait to care for those it damages. The Happy midi-narrative foreshortens hope, forgoing a vision of a better future for the world, for a better short-term future for ourselves as individual or families. This is not to say that young people lack integrity, or that they fail to live morally within their world view. Nor does it exonerate the Church from its failure to embody a full-blooded, life-affirming Christian faith, which young people could see and embrace. A re-engagement with Generation Y needs to be the fruit of repentance in the Church before it seeks repentance in the world.

'Young people's undergirding Happy midi-narrative is a celebration of this world, rather than an anticipation of the next' (see Chapter 7 above). Properly understood, Christian eschatology, rooted as it is in the Incarnation and the Resurrection, also offers the strongest grounds for the celebration of this life. But the anticipation of the next is also the anticipation of the world becoming more not less. A world- (that is, creation-)denying theology has no chance of engaging with Generation Y's world view. But Christianity is a world-celebrating faith. A vision of the renewed heaven and earth is a vital component of the Christian world view and an essential component of a Christian response to environmental concern.

World views are what the sociology of knowledge calls 'plausibility structures'. They make a particular view of life seem 'obvious' or plausible. 'The power of any culture is measured by the extent to which its formulation of reality seems "natural".'[16] 'Ideas and world views are maintained by social support. They are culturally embedded in community.'[17] 'We seldom live by ideas or ideologies but rather by images of life communicated by our surrounding worlds.'[18] Plausibility is closely linked to inevitability. If something seems 'natural' it must be right. St Paul says that 'the god of this world blinds minds' (2 Corinthians 4.4), where 'world' means the whole way of life apart from Christ. Culture, in other words, acts as a blindfold.

But if a positive alternative is on local display, then the plausibility of the original can be questioned. One of the saddest findings of this research was that 'Church is not seen by the majority of youth as a place of hope, just as an institution that is not the answer' (Chapter 1). We have to attend to our own plausibility, although our integrity is even more important. Andrew Walker has suggested the need for 'sectarian plausibility structures' to help maintain a grasp of the gospel in contemporary congregations.

> If the world staggers onwards with more consumption, wrapped up in mass culture yet splitting at the seams, we will need to *create sectarian plausibility structures* in order for our story to take hold of our congregations and root them in the gospel.[19]

By 'sectarian' he does not mean socially separated from society, but entered into voluntarily, as part of a deliberate choice to live differently. In an affluent culture like ours the Happy midi-narrative will seem sufficient and plausible unless it is shown to be deficient by something more appealing.

An adequate description of an appropriate plausible alternative would take another book, but we will revisit the different aspects of Wright's analysis of world views as a beginning.

'World views are like the foundations of a house: vital but invisible. They are that *through* which, not *at* which a society or individual normally looks; they form the grid through which humans organise reality.'[20] The difficulty with challenging a world view is precisely that most human beings organize reality this way without being aware of it. For most people a world view is 'obvious' or 'common sense' or simply 'The way we do things around here.' In other words, they are matters of faith. 'As a vision rooted in faith (any kind of faith) and experience, a world view in its basic tenets is not argued *to* but argued *from*.'[21]

Like an iceberg, most of a world view is below the surface, rather than visible to all. A lifestyle (praxis) is a world view made visible. Indeed the world view is to be read off the lifestyle, rather than vice versa. If there is a contradiction between people's description of their world view and their visible way of life, it is the description which is to be doubted. Within a relational approach, once mutual trust has been established, prior mission may well involve pointing out that people sometimes say one thing and do another. We may well be helping them to articulate their own story more accurately, or find ourselves challenging them as to whether they really wish to live the story that they claim to believe.

More important by far is the embodiment of a fuller, morally richer, life. The Happy midi-narrative is one-dimensional, compared with a vision of the kingdom of God. Censuring people for a way of life with which they are content, is a waste of time. But living in such a way that people are drawn to us and attracted by our way of life is at the heart of all mission.

The other 'above surface' dimension of a world view is symbolism. Some aspects of a shared way of life become iconic of the whole lifestyle and story. At one time the National Lottery logo and the words 'It could be you' gave a good indication as to where our society's heart lay. The iPod is symbolic of our individualized society, as well as part of its way of life, and so on. Ann Morisy has suggested that in some contexts we will have to teach people to use and recognize symbols as a resource for daily life. She is a long-standing advocate for 'apt liturgy'.[22] But we will also need to operate where 'liturgy' is not yet appropriate. The things that people aspire to reveal their hearts, they are iconic. Helping people to reflect on their 'icons', whether celebrities, the latest technology, or whatever, helps their reflection about the sort of person they want to be. There is also a theological connection to the theme of idolatry.

Once again we are challenged to offer an alternative, richer set of icons. But it will not suffice to introduce Christian symbolism into these conversations unless the symbols are genuinely integrated into our lives. The integrity of this sort of accompaniment will depend on what we are really seen as aspiring to.

Beneath the surface of a world view are both a story by which life is interpreted and a set of implied questions. The story is the real bottom line of a world view, but it is interdependent with the questions. One dimension of prior mission will involve helping people to identify the implicit questions they are seeking to answer. The Happy midi-narrative settles for too small a set of questions. Its story appears plausible because it does not ask the more difficult questions. Sometimes we may have to wait until life raises questions which the Happy midi-narrative cannot answer, but the challenge remains to live out the Christian story so that it attracts a new set of questions.

If we are to tell the gospel story effectively, we may need to develop another form of storytelling. Tom Wright has pointed out that Jesus' parables were 'ways of breaking open the world view of Jesus' hearers, so that it could be remoulded into the world view which he, Jesus, was commending'.[23] Jesus told stories that challenged the accepted stories of his day, and opened a window on an alternative one. Wright has pointed out that we have a long tradition of restaging the parables in contemporary form, from mystery plays to contemporary sketches. But we have not developed Jesus' skill of telling stories that undermine the controlling stories of our day, while simultaneously pointing to a better one. Subversive storytelling, like all the other dimensions of prior mission, requires the grace of the Holy Spirit if it is to be life giving.

The ministry of the Spirit

It is important to have appropriate theological and spiritual foundations for this work. The merely pragmatic will not do. What theological reasons are there to give hope that prior mission work could be effective? This requires a revisiting the concept of 'formative spirituality'.

As Bruce says, 'there is a simpler way of finding great reservoirs of religious sentiment in an apparently secular society: just rename the secular as religious! The broader the definition of religion, the more of it you will find.'[24] Is formative spirituality another rebranding, turning unbelief into belief? From the point of view of much of our society, the answer must be a qualified 'yes'. As this research has shown, those who have no belief in an identifiable, active God, have no transformative spirituality. Culture may have adopted the word 'spirituality' for everything from aromatherapy to attending to your inner self, but this has departed far from any recognizable Christian usage. The common use of the 'spirituality' word in our culture may establish some common ground, but if society in general and faith communities in particular mean something essentially different by it, the common ground will be decidedly narrow.

What, then, makes spirituality recognizable as spirituality, within the Christian tradition? The biblical answer is clear. It is the presence and activity of the Holy Spirit. The very word comes from a Greek term, seemingly coined by St Paul, to indicate the presence and activity of the Holy Spirit.[25] In one sense to speak of spirituality within the Christian tradition, has to be to speak of transformative spirituality. Theologically, spirituality is not a dimension or capacity within human beings. It is about the encounter with God for which humans are made. The Holy Spirit is not an impersonal immanent force, as in *Star Wars*, but the presence of the transcendent God. 'Talk of the Spirit is not a way of speaking of God's immanence, but of his transcendence. The Spirit may be active *within* the world, but he does not become a *part* of the world.'[26] The Spirit is 'God's empowering presence'.[27] In what way[s] then, might the Holy Spirit be active in formative spirituality?

Within the biblical tradition the Spirit is not limited to the work of redemption and its resulting spiritual growth. The Spirit is involved in the initial creation, bringing form to the formless, according to the word of God (Genesis 1). This role continues in the sustaining of creation (Psalm 104.27–30). The creation (whether its human stewards acknowledge it or not) is also in need of redemption. It is intended, through Christ, to become the new (renewed) creation. Paul connects the groaning of creation, in its need of release from bondage to decay, with the groaning of the Spirit over creation (Romans 8.19–27). As it is humans who give voice to creation's groaning, we may be confident that the Holy Spirit is at work whenever human beings begin to voice their concern at a broken earth and broken lives. As we encourage men and women to see beyond consumer complacency, the Spirit will be our mission leader.

The Spirit is the prior missioner par excellence. The Spirit worked in Cornelius, before bringing a reluctant evangelist out of his cultural comfort zone, to share with him.

> The Spirit is the Completer. Ultimately, the goal of the Spirit is to glorify the Father through the Son by bringing the Son's reign to completion ... His task is to effect the ultimate goal of God's program for creation.[28]

For that redemption purpose the Spirit is always ahead of the Church as it seeks to fulfil its mission. He is famously described by John Taylor as the 'Go-Between God', forging relationship with Christ, and enabling those who bear Christ to forge appropriate relationships with those for whom he also died.

We need to make a clear distinction between the personal indwelling of the Spirit in a believer, through baptism and conversion, and the work of the Spirit in bringing people to faith. Paul tells us that, 'the Spirit searches everything, even the depths of God', and asks 'what human being knows what is truly human except the human spirit that is within? So also no one comprehends what is truly God's except the Spirit of God' (1 Corinthians 2.11). The Spirit searches each human heart and longs to draw each one towards Christ.

We can, therefore, confidently expect the initiative, guidance and aid of the Holy Spirit in the task of prior mission. Human beings are made (formed by the Spirit) for relationship with God, which is made available in Christ. The Spirit reveals, convicts and converts. Wherever the members of Generation Y, and all those who think like them, may be, there, the Spirit of God is willing to meet them. It does not matter how far back we have to start.

Conclusion

Our research did not provide us with what we had hoped to find. It has, however, made a number of things very clear. There can be fruitful evangelistic work among both young people and adults now. It is going on, and it should continue. However the further we travel beyond those with any sort of contact with the Church, the further back we will have to start. We live in an instant culture, which cannot be reached by instant missionary tactics. There is no alternative to what we have called prior mission, and, even before that, to investment in real, long-term relationships. Patient loving and patient sowing will be the order of the day for years to come.

This also raises substantial challenges about the nature of our churches. Will they primarily be 'cities of refuge', defending their members from a rapidly changing culture? Or will they be disciple-making communities? Will they equip their members to engage with society as it is, not as they wish it to be. Can we also learn to value our society's strengths, as well as to grieve over its complacency and blindness? Above all, can we demonstrate a whole-life Christian discipleship which is both practical and attractive? 'Come to us' strategies will never bridge the gulf between church culture and the world view we have investigated. 'Go to' strategies are essential. The whole process would be greatly helped by the planting of new Christian communities, whether 'fresh expressions' or traditional in style, layered through society, and embodying the gospel as a viable alternative way of life.

The desire for happiness is entirely valid. Who wants to be unhappy? But authentic happiness, requires a meta-narrative, a full story which offers long-term hope, not a midi one focused on the immediate. The Happy midi-narrative will never be overturned by our criticism. It can only be outclassed by a Christlike way of life, for in him alone is true happiness to be found.

Appendix

Thumbnail sketch of the main *EastEnders* storylines at the time of interviewing

Trevor and Little Mo: Little Mo Morgan (née Slater) was suffering domestic violence at the hands of her husband Trevor. Despite numerous beatings and a rape she was loyal to him, but in the end fought back by hitting him with an iron. He survived. Little Mo went to jail for attempted murder.

Lisa and Phil: Lisa Fowler is married to Mark, a kind, hard-working man, if somewhat dull and lacking in ambition. Lisa has a baby (Louise) by 'hard man' publican Phil Mitchell, but she held off from telling him he is the father because of a complex and violent history between them. Mark had taken up the father role for Louise and had offered Lisa a stable family life. The attraction between Lisa and Phil, however, never completely goes away.

Kat and Zoë: Kat is one of the Slater sisters living with her father and 'Nan'. Zoë was brought up as Kat's sister, but Kat is really her mother, having been abused and become pregnant by her Uncle Harry as a teenager. Kat was forced to give up Zoë to the family and the abuse swept under the carpet. However, eventually the truth was revealed in a dramatic episode. Zoë, upset by the truth and knowledge of the cover-up, rejects Kat and runs away. Kat ends up trying to commit suicide but fails.

Phil and Steve: Phil Mitchell and Steve Owen are rivals and both are 'villains' in their own way. Phil is a 'hard man' generally dealing with things by way of physical violence. Steve is more of a wheeler-dealer businessman who does not like to get his hands dirty, but will call on others who do. Various payback attempts for past wrongs culminate in Steve taking Phil's baby (Louise), followed by a dramatic car chase as Phil tries to get her back. Steve crashes, Phil rescues Louise from the wrecked car, but Steve is trapped and the car explodes into flames, killing him.

Jamie and Sonia: Jamie Mitchell and Sonia Jackson are two younger characters in *EastEnders*. At the time of our interviews they were 'going out' together. Following an argument, however, Jamie slept with Janine Butcher, the local prostitute. Sonia was reluctant to take Jamie back, but he asked her to marry him. The engagement didn't last very long.

Notes

Chapter 1   Young people and the Church

1. Peter Brierley, *The Tide is Running Out: What the English Church Attendance Survey Reveals*, Christian Research, 2000, p. 99.
2. General Synod Board of Education, *Youth A Part*, Church House Publishing, 1996, p. 2.
3. For a comprehensive analysis of the concept of generations, see David Hilborn and Matt Bird (eds), *God and the Generations: Youth, Age and the Church Today*, Paternoster, 2002.
4. Karl Mannheim, 'The problem of generations', in *Essays on the Sociology of Knowledge*, Routledge & Kegan Paul, 1952, pp. 276–320.
5. The set of characteristics of these generations has been taken from Hilborn and Bird, *God and the Generations*. Birth years are approximate. Other scholars place them a few years earlier.
6. Hilborn and Bird, *God and the Generations*, p. 109.
7. Hilborn and Bird, *God and the Generations*, p. 119.
8. Hilborn and Bird, *God and the Generations*, p. 129.
9. Hilborn and Bird, *God and the Generations*, p. 140.
10. Chris Barker, *Television, Globalization and Cultural Identities*, Open University Press, 1999, p. 42.
11. Commenting on the work of Kenneth Roberts, *Youth and Employment in Modern Britain*, Oxford University Press, 1995, Harriet Bradley and Paul Hickman, 'In and out of work? The changing fortunes of young people in contemporary labour markets', in Jeremy Roche, Stanley Tucker, Rachel Thomson and Ronny Flynn (eds), *Youth in Society*, Sage Publications in association with The Open University, 2004, p. 127.
12. Madsen Pirie and Robert M. Worcester, *The Millennial Generation*, Adam Smith Institute, 1998.
13. Mannheim, 'The problem of generations'.
14. These include ballet, opera, classical concerts, etc.
15. Any contrast between popular culture and high culture in terms of aesthetic qualities is beyond our definition.
16. Brian J. Walsh and Richard J. Middleton, *The Transforming Vision*, InterVarsity Press, 1984, p. 35.

17. Wright later added a fifth question: 'What time is it?' See N. T. Wright, *Jesus and the Victory of God: Christian Origins and the Question of God*, SPCK, 1996, p. 138.
18. N. T. Wright, *The New Testament and the People of God: Christian Origins and the Question of God*, SPCK, 1992, p. 123.
19. Tom Beaudoin, *Virtual Faith: The Irreverent Spiritual Quest of Generation X*, Jossey-Bass Press, 1998, p. 21.
20. Stuart Rose, 'Is the term "spirituality" a word that everybody uses, but nobody knows what anyone means by it?', *Journal of Contemporary Religion* 16.2, 2001, pp. 193–207.
21. David Hay with Rebecca Nye, *The Spirit of the Child*, HarperCollins, 1998, p. 6.
22. Hay with Nye, *The Spirit of the Child*.
23. Thomas Luckmann, *The Invisible Religion: The Problem of Religion in Modern Society*, Macmillan, 1967.
24. Edward Bailey, *Implicit Religion: An Introduction*, Middlesex University Press, 1998.
25. National Youth Agency, *Spirituality and Spiritual Development in Youth Work: A Consultation Paper from the National Youth Agency*, The National Youth Agency, 2005.
26. Philip Sheldrake, *Spirituality and Theology: Christian Living and the Doctrine of God*, Darton, Longman & Todd, 1998, p. 35.
27. Hay with Nye, *The Spirit of the Child*.
28. Rose, 'The term "spirituality"', p. 204.
29. Paul Heelas and Linda Woodhead with Benjamin Seel, Bronislaw Szersznski and Karin Tusting, *The Spiritual Revolution: Why Religion is Giving Way to Spirituality*, Blackwell, 2005, p. 7.
30. Brierley, *The Tide*, p. 95.
31. Bob Jackson, *Hope for the Church: Contemporary Strategies for Growth*, Church House Publishing, 2002, p. 96.
32. Brierley, *The Tide*, p. 109.
33. Sylvia Collins, *Young People's Faith in Late Modernity*, University of Surrey, unpublished PhD Thesis, 1997. Leslie J. Francis, *The Values Debate: A Voice from the Pupils*, Woburn Press, 2001.
34. Philip Richter and Leslie J. Francis, *Gone but not Forgotten: Church Leaving and Returning*, Darton, Longman & Todd Ltd, 1998, p. 113.
35. Richter and Francis, *Gone but not Forgotten*, p. 63.
36. Francis, *The Values Debate*, p. 38.
37. David Day, '"Godliness and good learning": the role of the secondary school in the spiritual development of adolescent Christians', in Jeff Astley and David Day (eds), *The Contours of Christian Education*, McCrimmons, 1992, pp. 230–44.
38. Francis, *The Values Debate*, p. 166. This is more than the national average of 7.5

per cent for *Sunday* church attendance in 1998 (Brierley, *The Tide*, p. 9). Francis's sample consisted of 13- to 15-year-olds – some of their church attendance may have taken place on a different day of the week, and some may have been related to school activities. Young adults of 20–29 years old make up the smallest age group in Sunday church attendance, followed by 15- 19-year-olds.

39. Francis, *The Values Debate*, pp. 168, 172.
40. Jackson, *Hope for the Church*.
41. Danièle Hervieu-Léger, 'Religion, Memory and Catholic Identity: Young people in France and the "New Evangelisation of Europe"', in John Fulton and Peter Gee (eds), *Religion in Contemporary Europe*, Edwin Mellen Press, 1994, pp. 125–38.
42. Colleen Carroll, *The New Faithful: Why Young Adults are Embracing Christian Orthodoxy*, Loyola, 2002.
43. Jackson, *Hope for the Church*, p. 146.
44. Pete Ward, *Youthwork and the Mission of God*, SPCK, 1997.
45. Maxine Green and Chandu Christian, *Accompanying Young People on their Spiritual Quest*, Church House Publishing, 1998, p. 21.
46. Danny Brierley, *Joined Up*, Paternoster, 2003, p. 24.
47. Pete Ward, *Growing up Evangelical*, SPCK, 1996, p. 199.
48. Jackson, *Hope for the Church*, p. 104.

Chapter 2   Youth, religion and popular culture

1. Paul Heelas and Linda Woodhead with Benjamin Seel, Bronislaw Szersznski and Karin Tusting, *The Spiritual Revolution: Why Religion is Giving Way to Spirituality*, Blackwell, 2005.
2. Leslie J. Francis, *The Values Debate: A Voice from the Pupils*, Woburn Press, 2001, pp. 36, 40. This study is based on 33,000 13- 15-year-olds. (Because the figures are rounded up the total may exceed 100%.)
3. Sylvia Collins, *Young People's Faith in Late Modernity*, University of Surrey, unpublished PhD Thesis, 1997: a survey of 1096 English teenagers in the mid–1990s.
4. God still tends to be spoken of in masculine terms.
5. Grace Davie, *Religion in Britain Since 1945*, Blackwell, 1994, p. 1.
6. Philip Richter and Leslie J. Francis, *Gone but not Forgotten: Church Leaving and Returning*, Darton, Longman & Todd, 1998.
7. Danièle Hervieu-Léger, *Religion as a Chain of Memory*, Polity, 2000.
8. Mairi Levitt, *'Nice When They Are Young': Contemporary Christianity in Families and Schools*, Avebury, 1996.
9. Bob Mayo with Sara Savage and Sylvie Collins, *Ambiguous Evangelism*, SPCK, 2004.

10. J. Janssen, J. De Hart and M. Gerardts, 'Images of God in adolescence', *The International Journal for the Psychology of Religion* 4.2, 1994, pp. 105–21 (117).

11. D. Hutsebaut and D. Verhoeven, 'The adolescent's representation of God from age 12 to 18', *Journal of Empirical Theology* 4.1, 1991, pp. 59–72.

12. Grace Davie, *Religion in Modern Europe: A Memory Matters*, Oxford University Press, 2000.

13. Collins, *Young People's Faith in Late Modernity*, p. 78.

14. Danièle Hervieu-Léger, 'Present-day emotional renewals: The end of secularization or the end of religion?' in William H. Swatos Jr (ed.), *A Future for Religion?* Sage, 1993, pp. 129–48.

15. Kalvei Tamminem, 'Religious experiences in childhood and adolescence: A viewpoint of religious development between the ages of 7 and 20', *The International Journal for the Psychology of Religion* 4.2, 1994, pp. 61–85.

16. Heelas and Woodhead et al., *The Spiritual Revolution*, p. 107.

17. Francis, *The Values Debate*, p. 40.

18. Steve Collins, 'Church for a changing culture', *Alternativeworship.org* www.alternativeworship.org/theory_steve_music.html

19. Richard W. Flory and Donald E. Miller (eds), *GenX Religion*, Routledge, 2000.

20. Lori Jensen, Richard W. Flory and Donald E. Miller, 'Marked for Jesus: Sacred tattooing among evangelical GenXers', in Flory and Miller (eds), *GenX Religion*, pp. 15–30.

21. Arlene Sánchez Walsh, 'Slipping into darkness: Popular culture and the creation of a Latino evangelical youth culture', in Flory and Miller (eds), *GenX Religion*, pp. 74–91.

22. Kimberly Leaman Algallar and Richard W. Flory, 'Spirit made flesh: The tangible spirituality of "LL Prime Time"', in Flory and Miller (eds), *GenX Religion*, pp. 185–98.

23. Heidi Campbell, 'Approaches to religious research in computer-mediated communication', in Jolyon Mitchell and Sophia Marriage (eds), *Mediating Religion: Conversations in Media, Religion and Culture*, T&T Clark, 2003, pp. 213–28.

24. Joseph L. Price, 'An American apotheosis: Sports of popular religion', in Bruce David Forbes and Jeffrey H. Mahan (eds), *Religion and Popular Culture in America*, University of California Press, 2000, pp. 201–18.

25. Michael Jindra, 'It's about faith in our future: *Star Trek* fandom as cultural religion', in Forbes and Mahan (eds), *Religion and Popular Culture in America*, pp. 165–79.

26. Robert J. Higgs, 'Muscular Christianity, holy play and spiritual exercises: Confusion about Christ in sports and religion', *Arete* 1.1, 1983, pp. 59–85 (63), quoted at Forbes and Mahan (eds.), *Religion and Popular Culture in America*, p. 203.

27. Graham St John, 'The difference engine – liberation and the rave imaginary', in Graham St John (ed.), *Rave Culture and Religion*, Routledge, 2004, pp. 19–45.

28. Lynn Schofield Clark, *From Angels to Aliens: Teenagers, the Media and the Supernatural*, Oxford University Press, 2003.

29. Michael Ostling, 'Harry Potter and the disenchantment of the world', *Journal of Contemporary Religion* 18.1, 2003, pp. 3–24, and Clark, *From Angels to Aliens*, 2003, provide a commentary on this.

30. Collins, *Young People's Faith in Late Modernity*.

31. Rebecca Nye, 'Identifying the core of children's spirituality', in David Hay with Rebecca Nye, *The Spirit of the Child*, HarperCollins, 1998, pp. 112–37 (125).

32. Francis, *The Values Debate*, p. 193.

33. Clark, *From Angels to Aliens*, 2003.

34. Clark, *From Angels to Aliens*, p. 227.

35. Collins, *Young People's Faith in Late Modernity*.

36. Paul Willis, *Common Culture*, Open University Press, 1990, p. 135.

37. Steven Miles, *Youth Lifestyles in a Changing World*, Open University Press, 2000.

38. Michael E. Sobel, *Lifestyle and Social Structure: Concepts, Definitions, Analyses*, Academic Press, 1981, p. 171, quoted at Miles, *Youth Lifestyles*, p. 27.

39. Andrew M. Greeley, *God in Popular Culture*; Thomas More, 1988, quoted at Bruce Forbes, 'Introduction: Finding religion in unexpected places', in Forbes and Mahan (eds), *Religion and Popular Culture in America*, p. 12.

40. N. T. Wright, *The New Testament and the People of God: Christian Origins and the Question of God*, SPCK, 1992, p. 123.

41. Wright, *The New Testament*, p. 123.

42. N. T. Wright, *Jesus and the Victory of God: Christian Origins and the Question of God*, SPCK, 1996, p. 138.

43. Wright, *The New Testament*, p. 124.

44. Wright, *The New Testament*, p. 124.

45. Bath, Bristol, Cambridge, Colchester, Hitchin, Huddersfield, Ipswich, Kingston-upon-Thames, London, Nuneaton, Manchester, Marlow and Woodbridge. (Some towns contained more than one site.)

46. 17 and 25 people – while cumbersome to manage, these groups nevertheless yielded some useful data and were therefore retained in the study. In addition to the group interviews, there was also one individual interview.

47. *N4 Classic.* In order to analyse the data as comprehensively as possible, we adopted both a grounded-theory approach (Barney Glaser and Anselm Strauss, *The Discovery of Grounded Theory*, Weidenfeld & Nicolson, 1968) and a hypothesis-testing method. Grounded theory is a bottom-up method of data analysis that aims to give maximum expression to interviewees' ideas and comments. As far as possible during analysis, the researcher sets aside his or

her background knowledge, theoretical ideas and interests in order to look directly at the data on its own terms. This involves several stages of detailed coding to find relevant themes in the data. As we explored the themes we identified how they were constructed and related to one another, so we that we could begin to develop a theoretical understanding of the interviewees' thoughts and experiences.

A grounded approach is very effective in identifying themes that might otherwise have been missed in the analysis. However, it is a somewhat unstructured method that is, in part, dependent on the researcher's sensitivity to the data. We therefore decided to supplement our grounded analysis with another method that would be a little more standardized and purposive in terms of exploring preliminary hunches. In the case of image, following some grounded work, we returned to the psychological literature on conceptual categories and used this to formulate hypotheses which we then tested against our data. We expected that the bottom-up grounded theory and the top-down hypothesis testing methods would meet in the middle at similar conclusions. We were pleased when this turned out to be the case.

Throughout the research we have been careful to abide by the normal ethical practices of social research. In short, these state that the physical and emotional well-being of research participants must be safeguarded and that all research be conducted with professional integrity. We therefore followed the principles of voluntary participation and freely given, informed consent. Our interviewees knew the nature of our research before agreeing to take part and were competent enough to make their own decision as to the extent to which they participated in the group.

Chapter 3   Our findings: The Happy midi–narrative

1. Lynn Schofield Clark, *From Angels to Aliens: Teenagers, the Media and the Supernatural*, Oxford University Press, 2003.
2. All labels, such as the 'Happy midi-narrative', are simply convenient devices, which point towards a complex reality. Here, 'Happy' is a term that straddles the halfway point between the two senses of 'happiness' and 'happy-go-lucky' (the deep and shallow ends respectively), and, in our usage, encompasses both.
3. This borrows from Griemas's narrative structure used by Wright. See N. T. Wright, *The New Testament and the People of God: Christian Origins and the Question of God*, SPCK, 1992, pp. 70–7, quoting Algirdas Julien Griemas, *Sémantique Structurale*, Seuil, 1966; and *Due Sens*, Seuil, 1970.
4. Levi's *Odyssey* campaign, 2002.
5. It would seem that young people are not so burdened by the feelings of unacceptability that comes through guilt due to moral transgression, as from the shame of failing to live up to an ideal. Hence it may be that young people's

greatest *felt* need is for salvation from depression, which results from a failure to achieve happiness.

6. Wright, *The New Testament*.
7. Christian Smith with Melinda Lundquist Denton, *Soul Searching: The Religious and Spiritual Lives of American Teenagers*, Oxford University Press, 2005, p. 292.
8. Smith with Denton, *Soul Searching*, pp. 162–3.
9. Smith with Denton, *Soul Searching*, p. 163.
10. Smith with Denton, *Soul Searching*, p. 164.
11. Smith with Denton, *Soul Searching*, p. 165.
12. Sylvia Collins, *Young People's Faith in Late Modernity*, University of Surrey, unpublished PhD Thesis, 1997.
13. Smith with Denton, *Soul Searching*, pp. 127–8.
14. Collins, *Young People's Faith in Late Modernity*; eadem, 'Immanent faith: Young people in late modernity', in Leslie J. Francis, *Sociology, Theology and the Curriculum*, Cassell, 1999, pp. 165–74.
15. Collins, *Young People's Faith in Late Modernity*, p. 123.
16. Collins, *Young People's Faith in Late Modernity*, p. 134.
17. Collins, *Young People's Faith in Late Modernity*, p. 130.
18. Thomas Luckmann, *The Invisible Religion: The Problem of Religion in Modern Society*, Macmillan, 1967.
19. Martin Robinson, *The Faith of the Unbeliever*, Monarch, 1994.
20. Paul Heelas and Linda Woodhead with Benjamin Seel, Bronislaw Szersznski and Karin Tusting, *The Spiritual Revolution: Why Religion is Giving Way to Spirituality*, Blackwell, 2005.
21. Heelas and Woodhead, *The Spiritual Revolution*, p. 110.
22. Heelas and Woodhead, *The Spiritual Revolution*, suggest that on current trends this might happen in 30 years' time.

Chapter 4   Story through soaps and films

1. Bob Mayo with Sara Savage and Sylvie Collins, *Ambiguous Evangelism*, SPCK, 2004, pp. 80–2.
2. Throughout the chapter the term 'soaps' should be taken to mean 'British soaps' unless otherwise stated. Geraghty highlights some of the differences between British and American soaps. For example, British soaps such as *EastEnders*, *Coronation Street* and *Emmerdale* tend to have a much more 'domestic' feel compared to the more glamorous American soaps, such as *Dallas* and *Dynasty*, which were popular in the 1980s. See Christine Geraghty, *Women and Soap Opera*, Polity, 1991.
3. N. T. Wright, *The New Testament and the People of God: Christian Origins and the Question of God*, SPCK, 1992. Wright's 1996 question 'What time is it?' was

largely absent from the young people's comments. See Wright, *Jesus and the Victory of God: Christian Origins and the Question of God*, SPCK, 1996.

4. Paul Willis, *Common Culture*, Open University Press, 1990, p. 32.

5. David Buckingham, *Public Secrets:* EastEnders *and its Audience*, British Film Institute, 1987, p. 16.

6. Other films mentioned included: *Star Wars, The Idiots, Harry Potter, Top Gun, Bridget Jones' Diary, The Blair Witch Project, Terminator, Terminator II, Goodfellows, Pulp Fiction, Dogma, Titanic, The Matrix, Dead Poets Society, Trainspotting, Speed II, Close Encounters of the Third Kind, American Pie, Spiderman, Toy Story, Eyes Wide Shut, Charlie's Angels, Life of Brian, Moulin Rouge, Fast and Furious, Dirty Dancing, Schindler's List, Mission Impossible, Gosford Park, Good Will Hunting, Romeo and Juliet.*

7. The context in which the young people engage with the popular arts is very significant for how they are experienced. Watching a film alone at home is very different from watching it in a cinema with friends (our young people mainly talked about the latter). Equally, we found with music that the listening context is important for how it is heard and used (see Chapter 5).

8. Buckingham, *Public Secrets.*

9. Soap operas have always had to contend with a reputation for being second-rate. (Feminists have argued that this may have something to do with them being seen as a genre for women.) Ang (1985) in a study of *Dallas* audiences, found that people may explain their soap viewing habits with reference to this perception of soaps as television 'rubbish' – perhaps not watching them because they are perceived as low-grade entertainment produced for the indiscriminate consumption of a mindless population; or watching them, but with an ironic eye; or, finally, watching and enjoying the soap but justifying the choice to do so by acknowledging their reputation and then finding something good or worthwhile in them. See Ien Ang, *Watching Dallas*, Methuen, 1985.

10. Female role models were scarce in films: 'I kind of go, "Which women can I be?" and there aren't that many of them.' (Nicole).

11. Ang, *Watching Dallas*, quoted by John Storey, *Cultural Studies and the Study of Popular Culture: Theories and Methods*, Edinburgh University Press, 1996, p. 18.

12. Richard Dyer, 'Entertainment and utopia', in Rick Altman (ed.), *Genre: The Musical: A Reader*, Routledge & Kegan Paul, 1981, p. 177.

13. Christine Gledhill, 'Genre and gender: The case of soap opera', in Stuart Hall (ed.), *Representation: Cultural Representations and Signifying Practices*, Sage, 1997, pp. 337–86 (343).

14. Dyer, 'Entertainment and utopia'.

15. Geraghty, *Women and Soap Opera*. Jackie Stacey, *Star Gazing: Hollywood and Female Spectatorship*, Routledge, 1994.

16. Lisa was reluctant to tell Phil he was the father of her daughter Louise and, at

the time, she was living with Mark Fowler who was offering her and Louise a secure, if somewhat dull, family life. When Phil was finally told about Louise, Mark was reluctant for him to see the baby. The debate in the interviews revolved around whether Lisa should have told Phil about the baby and whether or not he should have access to her.

17. Sara Savage, 'Sculpting the Self', in Bob Mayo with Sara Savage and Sylvie Collins, *Ambiguous Evangelism*, SPCK, 2004, pp. 127–43.
18. Savage, 'Sculpting the Self'.
19. Paul Weston, 'Evangelicals and Evangelism', in I. Taylor (ed.), *Not Evangelical Enough! The Gospel at the Centre*, Paternoster, 2003, pp. 137–52.
20. C. Dykstra, *Vision and Character*, Paulist Press, 1981, p. 55.
21. Samuel Wells, *Improvisation: The Drama of Christian Ethics*, SPCK, 2004, pp. 55–7.

Chapter 5   Praxis through music and clubbing

1. Ben Malbon, *Clubbing: Clubbing Cultures and Experience*, Routledge, 1999.
2. Tom Beaudoin, *Virtual Faith: The Irreverent Spiritual Quest of Generation X*, Jossey-Bass Press, 1998.
3. N. T. Wright, *The New Testament and the People of God: Christian Origins and the Question of God*, SPCK, 1992, p. 124.
4. R. Murray Schafer, *The Tuning of the World*, Knopf, 1977.
5. These were: Iio's 'Rapture' (dance), Mary J. Blige's 'Family Affair' (R&B), The Streets' 'Pure Garage' (garage), Afroman's 'Because I Got High' (garage) and Faithless' 'Drifting Away' (house).
6. Dick Hebdige, *Subculture: The Meaning of Style*, Methuen, 1979; repr. 2001.
7. Beaudoin, *Virtual Faith*.
8. Gordon Lynch, *After Religion: 'Generation X' and the Search for Meaning*, Darton, Longman & Todd, 2002.
9. Andy Bennett, *Popular Music and Youth Culture: Music, Identity and Place*, Macmillan, 2000.
10. Simon Frith, *Performing Rites: Evaluating Popular Music*, Oxford University Press, 1998.
11. Malbon, *Clubbing*.
12. Paul Du Gay et al., *Doing Cultural Studies: The Story of the Sony Walkman*, Sage, 2000, p. 21.
13. Malbon, *Clubbing*, pp. 8, 18.
14. Malbon, *Clubbing*, p. 107.
15. Tim Olaveson, 'Connectedness and the rave experience – Rave as the new religious movement', in Graham St John (ed.), *Rave Culture and Religion*, Routledge, 2004, pp. 85–106.
16. Paul Heelas, 'Introduction: on differentiation and dedifferentiation', in Paul Heelas, *Religion, Modernity and Postmodernity*, Blackwell, 1998, p. 5.

17. Bennett, *Popular Music and Youth Culture*.
18. Nicholas Saunders, Anja Saunders and Michelle Pauli, *In Search of the Ultimate High: Spiritual Experience through Psychoactives*, Rider, 2000.
19. A. Petridis, 'Bored of the dance', *Guardian*, 3 November 2004.
20. Malbon, *Clubbing*, p. 164.
21. Angela McRobbie, *In the Culture Society: Art, Fashion and Popular Music*, Routledge, 1999.

Chapter 6 Symbol through cultural icons and advertising images

1. N. T. Wright, *The New Testament and the People of God: Christian Origins and the Question of God*, SPCK, 1992.
2. For example, Eleanor Rosch, 'Principles of Categorisation', in Eleanor Rosch and Barbara Lloyd (eds), *Cognition and Categorisation*, Lawrence Erlbaum Associates, 1978 pp. 27–48; Lawrence Barsalou and Douglas Medin, 'Concepts: Fixed definitions or dynamic context-dependent representations', *Cahiers de Psychologie Cognitive* 6, 1986, pp. 187–202; Robert Nosofsky, 'Exemplar-based accounts of relations between classifications, recognition, and typicality', *Journal of Experimental Psychology: Learning, Memory and Cognition* 14, 1988, pp. 700–708.
3. K. Anders Ericsson and Herbert Simon, *Protocol Analysis: Verbal Reports as Data*, MIT Press, 1984.
4. Milton Rokeach, *The Open and Closed Mind*, Basic Books, 1960.
5. Sara Savage, 'A psychology of fundamentalism: the search for inner failings', in Martyn Percy (ed.), *Fundamentalism, Church and Society*, SPCK, 2002, pp. 25–52.
6. Seventy-six per cent of total thinking is open with contradictory (social) images; 83 per cent is open with 4 contradictory (intra-individual) images.
7. Semir Zeki, 'Neural concept formation and art', *Journal of Consciousness Studies* 9.3, 2002, pp. 53–76.
8. Schopenhauer, 1859, as cited by Zeki, 'Neural concept formation and art'.
9. Bob Mayo with Sara Savage and Sylvie Collins, *Ambiguous Evangelism*, SPCK, 2004.

Chapter 7 The world view of Generation Y: Implications for Christian–based youth work

1. Ann Morisy, 'Serving society – building disciples', in Steven Croft (ed.), *The Future of the Parish System*, Church House Publishing, 2006.
2. Christian Smith with Melinda Lundquist Denton, *Soul Searching: The Religious and Spiritual Lives of American Teenagers*, Oxford University Press, 2005, pp. 260, 266.
3. For a view of some of these, see www.alt-worship.org/altg.html

4. See www.freshexpressions.org.uk
5. Fraser Watts, 'Interacting cognitive subsystems and religious meanings', in R. Joseph (ed.), *Neurotheology: Brain, Science, Spirituality, Religious Experience*, California University Press, 2002, pp. 183–8.
6. Watts, 'Interacting cognitive subsystems and religious meanings'.
7. David Bosch, *Transforming Mission*, Orbis, 2003.
8. Lesslie Newbigin, *The Gospel in a Pluralist Society*, SPCK, 1989, p. 152.
9. www.silverringthing.com.
10. Marshall McLuhan, *Understanding Media: The Extensions of Man*, Routledge & Kegan Paul, 1964.
11. Lesslie Newbigin, *The Other Side of 1984: Questions for the Churches*, WCC Publications, 1983, p. 151.
12. Laurence Steinberg, Nancy Darling and Anne Fletcher, 'Authoritative parenting and adolescent adjustment: An ecological journey', in Glen Elder Jr and Phyllis Moen (eds), *Examining Lives in Context: Perspectives on the Ecology of Human Development*, American Psychological Association, 1995, pp. 423–66.
13. Sara Savage, 'Psychological perspectives on the present situation for clergy and congregations', in Steven Croft (ed.), *The Future of the Parish System*, Church House Publishing, 2006.
14. Aristotle, *Nicomachean Ethics*, translated and edited by Roger Crisp, Cambridge University Press, 2000.
15. Kerry Young, *The Art of Youth Work*, Russell House, 1999, p. 2.
16. Sarah Banks, *Ethical Issues in Youth Work*, Routledge, 1999.
17. Alisdair MacIntyre, *After Virtue*, Duckworth, 1985, p. 22.
18. Allan Bloom, *The Closing of the American Mind*, Penguin, 1987.

Chapter 8 Making disturbing sense of Generation Y

1. See the work of Grace Davie, David Lyon, Robin Gill and others.
2. Paul Heelas and Linda Woodhead et al., *The Spiritual Revolution: Why Religion is Giving Way to Spirituality*, Blackwell, 2005, p. 70.
3. Charles Taylor, *The Ethics of Authenticity*, Harvard University Press, 1991, p. 26.
4. John Drane, *The McDonaldization of the Church*, Darton, Longman & Todd, 2000, pp. 60–79.
5. Heelas and Woodhead et al., *The Spiritual Revolution*, p. x.
6. Rob Frost, *Essence: Exploring Spirituality*, Kingsway/CPAS, 2002.
7. Heelas and Woodhead et al., *The Spiritual Revolution*, pp. 107–10, 134.
8. See the Government statistics web site, www.nationalstatistics.gov.uk.
9. Grace Davie, *Religion in Britain since 1945: Believing Without Belonging*, Blackwell, 1994.
10. Grace Davie, *Religion in Modern Europe: A Memory Mutates*, Oxford, 2000.

11. José Casanova, *Public Religions in the Modern World*, University of Chicago Press, 1994.
12. Robin Gill, *Church Going and Christian Ethics*, Cambridge University Press, 1999, ch. 3.
13. Gill, *Church Going and Christian Ethics*, p. 85.
14. The Economic and Social Research Council, The University of Manchester, *The British Household Study and Key Issues in Religious Change*, 2005.
15. University of Manchester web site press release: www.manchester.ac.uk/press/title,38696,en.htm
16. *Mission-shaped Church: Church Planting and Fresh Expressions of Church in a Changing Context*, Church House Publishing, 2004, pp. 36–41.
17. Zygmunt Bauman, *Society Under Siege*, Polity, 2002, p. 21.
18. Tex Sample, *The Spectacle of Worship in a Wired World*, Abingdon, 1998, p. 42.
19. Steven Miles, *Youth Lifestyles in a Changing World*, Open University Press, 2000, p. 147.
20. Walter Truett Anderson, *The Fontana Post-Modernism Reader*, Fontana, 1995, pp. 2ff.
21. David Lyon, *Jesus in Disneyland*, Polity, 2000, p. 7. See also his *Postmodernity*, 2nd edn, Open University Press, 1999.
22. Because the term is still in academic use, and has been prolific in recent academic publishing, it is inevitable that I use some quotations and references that still use it.
23. Zygmunt Bauman and Keith Tester, *Conversations with Zygmunt Bauman*, Polity, 2001, p. 128.
24. Lyon, *Jesus in Disneyland*, p. 7.
25. Zygmunt Bauman, *Work, Consumerism and the New Poor*, Open University Press, 1998, p. 24.
26. David Lyon, 'Memory and the Millennium', in T. Bradshaw (ed.), *Grace and Truth in the Secular Age*, Eerdmans, 1998, p. 284.
27. Yiannis Gabriel and Tim Lang, *The Unmanageable Consumer*, Sage, 1995, p. 27.
28. Grace Davie, 'From obligation to consumption: patterns of religion in Northern Europe at the start of the twenty-first century', Bishop's Day Conference, 4 September 2002, The Diocese of St Albans web site: www.stalbans.anglican.org/daviepres.htm
29. Davie, 'From obligation to consumption'.
30. George Ritzer, *Enchanting a Disenchanted World*, Pine Forge, 1999, p. 36.
31. Steven Miles, *Consumerism as a Way of Life*, Sage, 1998, p. 1.
32. Gabriel and Lang, *The Unmanageable Consumer*, p. 100.
33. See in particular Colin Campbell, *The Romantic Ethic and the Spirit of Modern Consumerism*, Alcuin Academics, 1987; repr. 2005.
34. Lyon, 'Memory and the Millennium', p. 285.

35. Lyon, *Jesus in Disneyland*, p. 13.
36. Charles Jencks, *What Is Postmodernism?* Academy Editions, 1986, p. 43.
37. Dick Hebdige, *Hiding in the Light*, Routledge, 1988, p. 210.
38. Kenneth Gergen, *An Invitation to Social Construction*, Sage, 1999, p. 2.
39. Don Tapscott, *Growing Up Digital*, McGraw-Hill, 1998, p. 26.
40. Sherry Turkle, *Life on the Screen*, Phoenix, 1997, p. 10.
41. David Buckingham, *After the Death of Childhood – Growing Up in the Age of Electronic Media*, Polity, 2000, p. 80.
42. David Lyon, 'Hazard Warning', *Third Way* 17.8, October 1994, pp. 22–5.
43. Richard Bauckham and Trevor Hart, *Hope Against Hope*, Darton, Longman & Todd, 1999, p. 58.
44. Chris Abbott, 'Making connections: young people and the Internet', in Julian Sefton-Green (ed.), *Digital Diversions*, University College London, 1998, pp. 85–6.
45. Abbott, 'Making connections'.
46. Michael Welker, *God the Spirit*, Fortress, 1994, p. 29.
47. Sample, *The Spectacle of Worship in a Wired World*, p. 15.
48. Andrew Walker, *Telling the Story*, SPCK, 1996, p. 197.
49. See Manuel Castells, *The Rise of the Network Society*, 2nd edn, Blackwell, 2000.
50. Mark Poster, 'Postmodern Virtualities', in Mike Featherstone and Roger Burrows (eds), *Cyberspace, Cyberbodies, Cyberpunk*, Sage, 1995, pp. 79–95 (79).
51. Castells, *The Rise of the Network Society*.
52. Roland Robertson, *Globalization*, Sage, 1992, p. 8.
53. Anthony Giddens, *Runaway World*, Profile, 1999, p. 4.
54. John Tomlinson, *Globalization and Culture*, Polity, 1999, p. 29.
55. Lyon, *Jesus in Disneyland*, p. 11.
56. Paul Virilio, in John Armitage (ed.), *Virilio Live: Selected Interviews*, Sage, 2001, p. 80.
57. Zygmunt Bauman, *Life in Fragments*, Blackwell, 1995, p. 5.
58. Lyon, *Jesus in Disneyland*, p. 12.
59. Lyon, *Jesus in Disneyland*, p. 123.
60. See Tom Beaudoin, *Virtual Faith*, Jossey-Bass, 1998; and Richard W. Flory and Donald E. Miller (eds), *GenX Religion*, Routledge, 2000.
61. Andy Furlong and Fred Cartmel, *Young People and Social Change*, Open University Press, 1997, p. 5.
62. Taylor, *The Ethics of Authenticity*, p. 26.
63. See Ulrich Beck and Elisabeth Beck-Gernsheim, *Individualization*, Sage, 2002.
64. Ulrich Beck, *Risk Society*, Sage, 1992, p. 135.
65. E.g., Robert Putnam, *Bowling Alone*, Simon & Schuster, 2000.
66. Beck, *Risk Society*, p. 137.
67. Anthony Giddens, *Modernity and Self-Identity*, Polity, 1991, p. 5.

68. Lyon, 'Memory and the Millennium', p. 284.
69. Giddens, *Modernity and Self-Identity*, p. 199.
70. Lyon, *Jesus in Disneyland*, p. 12.
71. Lyon, *Jesus in Disneyland*, p. 69.
72. Richard Rorty, *Contingency Irony and Solidarity*, Cambridge University Press, 1989, pp. 83ff.
73. Kieran Flanagan, *The Enchantment of Sociology*, Macmillan, 1999, p. 32.
74. Christoph Schwöbel, 'God, Creation and the Christian Community', in Colin Gunton (ed.), *The Doctrine of Creation*, T&T Clark, 1997, pp. 167ff.
75. Sherry Turkle, *Life On the Screen*, Phoenix, 1997, p. 10.
76. Lyon, *Jesus in Disneyland*, p. 95.
77. See Zygmunt Bauman, *Liquid Modernity*, Polity, 2000, pp. 49ff.
78. Lyon, *Jesus in Disneyland*, p. 69.
79. Bauman, *Life in Fragments*, p. 89.
80. Iain Chambers, 'Cities Without Maps', in Jon Bird, Barry Curtis, Tim Putnam, George Robertson and Lisa Tickner (eds), *Mapping the Futures*, Routledge, 1993, pp. 188–98 (193).
81. See Andrew Calcutt, *Arrested Development: Pop Culture and the Erosion of Adulthood*, Cassell, 1998.
82. See my *Postmodern Culture and Youth Discipleship*, Grove Pastoral Series 76, 1998; Furlong and Cartmel, *Young People and Social Change*; Miles, *Youth Lifestyles in a Changing World*.
83. Sample, *The Spectacle of Worship in a Wired World*, pp. 121–2.

Chapter 9 Reconnecting with Generation Y – and all those like them

1. Andy Furlong and Fred Cartmel, *Young People and Social Change*, Open University Press, 1997; Steven Miles, *Youth Lifestyles in a Changing World*, Open University Press, 2000.
2. *Mission-shaped Church: Church Planting and Fresh Expressions of Church in a Changing Context*, Church House Publishing, 2004, pp. 40–1.
3. *Mission-shaped Church*, pp. 36–9.
4. John Drane, *The MacDonaldization of the Church*, Darton, Longman & Todd, 2000, ch. 4.
5. E.g. The Institute for Theology, Imagination and the Arts at the University of St Andrews, www.st-andrews.ac.uk/institutes/itia, Theology Through the Arts at Ridley Hall, Cambridge (and St Andrews), www.theolarts.org, and the Images of Salvation resource published by the Christianity and Culture Project run jointly by the Centre for Medieval Studies, York, and St John's College, Nottingham, www.york.ac.uk/inst/cms/candc/projinfo.html. See also the 'Sense Making Faith' materials due to be published by MTAG.
6. See Grace Davie, *Religion in Modern Europe: A Memory Mutates*, Oxford, 2000, pp. 177–8.

7. Andrew Walls, *The Missionary Movement in Christian History*, T&T Clark, 1996, p. 258.

8. *Mission-shaped Church*, pp. 87–93.

9. Tex Sample, *The Spectacle of Worship in a Wired World*, Abingdon, 1998, p. 105.

10. Ann Morisy, *Journeying Out*, Continuum, 2004.

11. Morisy, *Journeying Out*, p. 154.

12. Morisy, *Journeying Out*, p. 154.

13. Graham Tomlin, *The Provocative Church*, SPCK, 2002.

14. David Runcorn, *Choice, Desire and the Will of God*, SPCK, 2003, p. 70.

15. See Furlong and Cartmel, *Young People and Social Change*, ch. 6; and The Henley Centre, *The Burden of Youth*, a report commissioned by the Salvation Army, available on the Salvation Army web site: www.salvationarmy.org.uk/uki/ www_uki.nsf/vw-search/ 269310A2600447B480256F9700534B73?opendocument

16. James Hunter, 'What is Modernity?' in Philip Sampson, Vinay Samuel and Christopher Sugden (eds), *Faith and Modernity*, Regnum, 1994, p. 13.

17. Andrew Walker, *Telling the Story*, SPCK, 1996, p. 124.

18. Michael Paul Gallagher, *Clashing Symbols*, Darton, Longman & Todd, 1997, pp. 4–5.

19. Walker, *Telling the Story*, p. 190.

20. N. T. Wright, *The New Testament and the People of God: Christian Origins and the Question of God*, SPCK, 1992, p. 125.

21. David Bosch, *Believing in the Future*, Gracewing, 1995, p. 49.

22. Morisy, *Journeying Out*, pp. 156–68.

23. Wright, *The New Testament and the People of God*, p. 77; *Jesus and the Victory of God: Christian Origins and the Question of God*, SPCK, 1996, pp. 174–82.

24. Steve Bruce, *God Is Dead: Secularization in the West*, Blackwell, 2002, p. 199.

25. See Gordon Fee, *Listening to the Spirit in the Text*, Eerdmans, 2000, ch. 4.

26. Colin Gunton, 'The Spirit in the Trinity', in Alasdair Heron and Colin Davey (eds), *The Forgotten Trinity*, CCBI, 1991, p. 123.

27. Gordon Fee, *God's Empowering Presence*, Baker, 1994.

28. Stanley Grenz, *Theology for the Community of God*, Paternoster, 1994, pp. 490–91.

Bibliography

Chris Abbott, 'Making connections: Young people and the Internet', in Julian Sefton-Green (ed.), *Digital Diversions*, University College London, 1998.

Kimberly Leaman Algallar and Richard W. Flory, 'Spirit made flesh: The tangible spirituality of "LL Prime Time"', in Richard W. Flory and Donald E. Miller (eds), *GenX Religion*, Routledge, 2000.

Walter Truett Anderson, *The Fontana Post-Modernism Reader*, Fontana, 1995.

Ien Ang, *Watching Dallas*, Methuen, 1985.

Aristotle, *Nicomachean Ethics*, translated and edited by Roger Crisp, Cambridge University Press, 2000.

Edward Bailey, *Implicit Religion: An Introduction*, Middlesex University Press, 1998.

Sarah Banks, *Ethical Issues in Youth Work*, Routledge, 1999.

Chris Barker, *Television, Globalization and Cultural Identities*, Open University Press, 1999.

Lawrence Barsalou and Douglas Medin, 'Concepts: Fixed definitions or dynamic context-dependent representations', *Cahiers de Psychologie Cognitive* 6, 1986, pp. 187–202.

Richard Bauckham and Trevor Hart, *Hope Against Hope*, Darton, Longman & Todd, 1999.

Zygmunt Bauman, *Society Under Siege*, Polity, 2002.

— *Liquid Modernity*, Polity, 2000.

— *Work, Consumerism and the New Poor*, Open University Press, 1998.

—— *Life in Fragments*, Blackwell, 1995.

Zygmunt Bauman and Keith Tester, *Conversations with Zygmunt Bauman*, Polity, 2001.

Tom Beaudoin, *Virtual Faith: The Irreverent Spiritual Quest of Generation X*, Jossey-Bass Press, 1998.

Ulrich Beck, *Risk Society*, Sage, 1992.

Ulrich Beck and Elisabeth Beck-Gernsheim, *Individualization*, Sage, 2002.

Andy Bennett, *Popular Music and Youth Culture: Music, Identity and Place*, Macmillan, 2000.

Allan Bloom, *The Closing of the American Mind*, Penguin, 1987.

David Bosch, *Transforming Mission*, Orbis, 2003.

—— *Believing in the Future*, Gracewing, 1995.

Harriet Bradley and Paul Hickman, 'In and out of work? The changing fortunes of young people in contemporary labour markets', in Jeremy Roche et al. (eds), *Youth in Society*, Sage Publications in association with The Open University, 2004.

Danny Brierley, *Joined Up*, Paternoster, 2003.

Peter Brierley, *The Tide is Running Out: What the English Church Attendance Survey Reveals*, Christian Research, 2000.

Steve Bruce, *God Is Dead: Secularization in the West*, Blackwell, 2002.

David Buckingham, *After the Death of Childhood: Growing Up in the Age of Electronic Media*, Polity, 2000.

—— *Public Secrets:* EastEnders *and its Audience*, British Film Institute, 1987.

Andrew Calcutt, *Arrested Development: Pop Culture and the Erosion of Adulthood*, Cassell, 1998.

Colin Campbell, *The Romantic Ethic and the Spirit of Modern Consumerism*, Alcuin Academics, 1987.

Heidi Campbell, 'Approaches to religious research in computer-mediated communication', in Jolyon Mitchell and Sophia Marriage (eds), *Mediating Religion: Conversations in Media, Religion and Culture*, T&T Clark, 2003.

Colleen Carroll, *The New Faithful: Why Young Adults are Embracing Christian Orthodoxy*, Loyola Press, 2002.

José Casanova, *Public Religions in the Modern World*, University of Chicago Press, 1994.

Manuel Castells, *The Rise of the Network Society*, 2nd edn, Blackwell, 2000.

Iain Chambers, 'Cities Without Maps', in Jon Bird et al. (eds), *Mapping the Futures*, Routledge, 1993, pp. 188–98.

Lynn Schofield Clark, *From Angels to Aliens: Teenagers, the Media and the Supernatural*, Oxford University Press, 2003.

Steve Collins, *Church for a Changing Culture* www.alternativeworship.org/theory_steve_music.html (accessed 6 April 2005)

Sylvia Collins, *Young People's Faith in Late Modernity*, University of Surrey, unpublished PhD Thesis, 1997.

— 'Immanent faith: Young people in late modernity', in Leslie J. Francis (ed.), *Sociology, Theology and the Curriculum*, Cassell, 1999, pp. 165–74.

Graham Cray, *Postmodern Culture and Youth Discipleship*, Grove Pastoral Series 76, 1998.

Grace Davie, 'From obligation to consumption: patterns of religion in Northern Europe at the start of the twenty-first century', Bishop's Day Conference, 4 September 2002, The Diocese of St Albans web site (online article www.stalbans.anglican.org/daviepres.htm).

— *Religion in Modern Europe: A Memory Mutates*, Oxford, 2000.

— *Religion in Britain since 1945: Believing Without Belonging*, Blackwell, 1994.

David Day, ' "Godliness and good learning": The role of the secondary school in the spiritual development of adolescent Christians', in Jeff Astley and David Day (eds), *The Contours of Christian Education*, McCrimmons, 1992.

Paul du Gay et al., *Doing Cultural Studies: The Story of the Sony Walkman*, Sage, 2000.

Richard Dyer, 'Entertainment and utopia', in Rick Altman (ed.), *Genre: The Musical: A Reader*, Routledge & Kegan Paul, 1981.

C. Dykstra, *Vision and Character*, Paulist Press, 1981.

The Economic and Social Research Council, The University of Manchester, *The British Household Study and Key Issues in Religious Change*, 2005.

K. Anders Ericsson and Herbert Simon, *Protocol Analysis: Verbal Reports as Data*, MIT Press, 1984.

Gordon Fee, *Listening to the Spirit in the Text*, Eerdmans, 2000.

— *God's Empowering Presence*, Baker, 1994.

Kieran Flanagan, *The Enchantment of Sociology*, Macmillan, 1999.

Richard W. Flory and Donald E. Miller (eds), *GenX Religion*, Routledge, 2000.

Bruce Forbes, 'Introduction: Finding religion in unexpected places', in Bruce Forbes and Jeffrey Mahan (eds), *Religion and Popular Culture in America*, University of California Press, 2000, pp. 1–20.

Leslie J. Francis, *The Values Debate: A Voice from the Pupils*, Woburn Press, 2001.

Simon Frith, *Performing Rites: Evaluating Popular Music*, Oxford University Press, 1998.

Rob Frost, *Essence: Exploring Spirituality*, Kingsway/CPAS, 2002.

Andy Furlong and Fred Cartmel, *Young People and Social Change*, Open University Press, 1997.

Yiannis Gabriel and Tim Lang, *The Unmanageable Consumer*, Sage, 1995.

Michael Paul Gallagher, *Clashing Symbols*, Darton, Longman & Todd, 1997.

General Synod Board of Education, *Youth A Part*, Church House Publishing, 1996.

Christine Geraghty, *Women and Soap Opera*, Polity, 1991.

Kenneth Gergen, *An Invitation to Social Construction*, Sage, 1999.

Anthony Giddens, *Runaway World*, Profile, 1999.

— *Modernity and Self-Identity*, Polity, 1991.

Robin Gill, *Church Going and Christian Ethics*, Cambridge University Press, 1999.

Barney Glaser and Anselm L. Strauss, *Discovery of Grounded Theory*, Aldine De Gruyter, 1967.

Christine Gledhill, 'Genre and gender: The case of soap opera', in Stuart Hall (ed.), *Representation: Cultural Representations and Signifying Practices*, Sage, 1997, pp. 337–86.

Andrew M. Greeley, *God in Popular Culture*, Thomas More Press, 1988.

Maxine Green and Chandu Christian, *Accompanying Young People on Their Spiritual Quest*, Church House Publishing, 1998.

Stanley Grenz, *Theology for the Community of God*, Paternoster, 1994.

Algirdas Julien Griemas, *Sémantique Structurale*, Seuil, 1966.

— *Due Sens*, Seuil, 1970.

Colin Gunton, 'The Spirit in the Trinity', in Alasdair Heron and Colin Davey (eds), *The Forgotten Trinity*, CCBI, 1991, pp. 123–35.

David Hay with Rebecca Nye, *The Spirit of the Child*, HarperCollins, 1998.

Dick Hebdige, *Hiding in the Light*, Routledge, 1988.

— *Subculture: The Meaning of Style*, Methuen, 1979; repr. 2001.

Paul Heelas, 'Introduction: On differentiation and dedifferentiation', in Paul Heelas, *Religion, Modernity and Postmodernity*, Blackwell, 1998, pp. 1–18.

Paul Heelas and Linda Woodhead et al., *The Spiritual Revolution: Why Religion is Giving Way to Spirituality*, Blackwell, 2005.

Danièle Hervieu-Léger, 'Present-day emotional renewals: The end of secularization or the end of religion?' in William H. Swatos Jr (ed.), *A Future for Religion?*, Sage, 1993, pp. 129–48.

— 'Religion, Memory and Catholic Identity: Young people in France and the "New Evangelisation of Europe"', in John Fulton and Peter Gee (eds), *Religion in Contemporary Europe*, Edwin Mellen Press, 1994, pp. 125–38.

Danièle Hervieu-Léger, *Religion as a Chain of Memory*, Polity, 2000.

Robert J. Higgs, 'Muscular Christianity, holy play and spiritual exercises: Confusion about Christ in sports and religion', *Arete* 1.1, 1983, pp. 59–85 (63) quoted at Bruce Forbes and Jeffrey Mahan (eds), *Religion and Popular Culture in America*, University of California Press, 2000, p. 203.

David Hilborn and Matt Bird (eds), *God and the Generations: Youth, Age and the Church Today*, Paternoster, 2002.

James Hunter, 'What is Modernity?' in Philip Sampson, Vinay Samuel and Christopher Sugden (eds), *Faith and Modernity*, Regnum, 1994, pp. 12–28.

D. Hutsebaut and D. Verhoeven, 'The adolescent's representation of God from age 12 to 18', *Journal of Empirical Theology* 4.1, 1991, pp. 59–72.

Bob Jackson, *Hope for the Church: Contemporary Strategies for Growth*, Church House Publishing, 2002.

J. Janssen, J. De Hart and M. Gerardts, 'Images of God in adolescence', *The International Journal for the Psychology of Religion* 4.2, 1994, pp. 105–21.

Charles Jencks, *What Is Postmodernism?* Academy Editions, 1986.

Lori Jensen, Richard W. Flory and Donald E. Miller, 'Marked for Jesus: Sacred tattooing among evangelical GenXers', in Richard W. Flory and Donald E. Miller (eds), *GenX Religion*, Routledge, 2000, pp. 15–30.

Michael Jindra, 'It's about faith in our future: *Star Trek* fandom as cultural religion', in Bruce David Forbes and Jeffrey H. Mahan (eds), *Religion and Popular Culture in America*, University of California Press, 2000, pp. 165–79.

Mairi Levitt, *'Nice When They Are Young': Contemporary Christianity in Families and Schools*, Avebury, 1996.

Thomas Luckmann, *The Invisible Religion: The Problem of Religion in Modern Society*, Macmillan, 1967.

Gordon Lynch, *After Religion: 'Generation X' and the Search for Meaning*, Darton, Longman & Todd, 2002.

David Lyon, *Jesus in Disneyland*, Polity, 2000.

— *Postmodernity*, 2nd edn, Open University Press, 1999.

— 'Memory and the Millennium', in T. Bradshaw (ed.), *Grace and Truth in the Secular Age*, Eerdmans, 1998, pp. 279–94.

Alisdair MacIntyre, *After Virtue*, Duckworth, 1985.

Ben Malbon, *Clubbing: Clubbing Cultures and Experience*, Routledge, 1999.

Karl Mannheim, 'The problem of generations', *Essays on the Sociology of Knowledge*, Routledge & Kegan Paul, 1952, pp. 276–320.

Bob Mayo with Sara Savage and Sylvie Collins, *Ambiguous Evangelism*, SPCK, 2004.

Marshall McLuhan, *Understanding Media: The Extentions of Man*, Routledge & Kegan Paul, 1964.

Angela McRobbie, *In the Culture Society: Art, Fashion and Popular Music*, Routledge, 1999.

Steven Miles, *Youth Lifestyles in a Changing World*, Open University Press, 2000.

Mission and Public Affairs Council, *Mission-shaped Church: Church Planting and Fresh Expressions of Church in a Changing Context*, Church House Publishing, 2004.

Ann Morisy, 'Serving society – building disciples', in Steven Croft (ed.), *The Future of the Parish System*, Church House Publishing, 2006.

National Youth Agency, *Spirituality and Spiritual Development in Youth Work:*

A Consultation Paper from the National Youth Agency, National Youth Agency, 2005.

—— *Towards a Core Curriculum – the Next Step: Report of the Second Ministerial Conference*, National Youth Bureau, 1991.

Lesslie Newbigin, *The Gospel in a Pluralist Society*, SPCK, 1989.

—— *The Other Side of 1984: Questions for the Churches*, WCC Publications, 1983.

Robert Nosofsky, 'Exemplar-based accounts of relations between classifications, recognition, and typicality', *Journal of Experimental Psychology: Learning, Memory and Cognition* 14, 1988, pp. 700–708.

Rebecca Nye, 'Identifying the core of children's spirituality', in David Hay with Rebecca Nye, *The Spirit of the Child*, HarperCollins, 1998, pp. 112–37.

Tim Olaveson, 'Connectedness and the rave experience – Rave as the new religious movement', in Graham St John (ed.), *Rave Culture and Religion*, Routledge, 2004, pp. 85–106.

Michael Ostling, 'Harry Potter and the disenchantment of the world', *Journal of Contemporary Religion* 18.1, 2003, pp. 3–23.

A. Petridis, 'Bored of the dance', *Guardian*, 3 November 2004.

Madsen Pirie and Robert M. Worcester, *The Millennial Generation*, Adam Smith Institute, 1998.

Mark Poster, 'Postmodern Virtualities', in Mike Featherstone and Roger Burrows (eds), *Cyberspace, Cyberbodies, Cyberpunk*, Sage, 1995, pp. 79–95.

Joseph L. Price, 'An American apotheosis: Sports of popular religion', in Bruce David Forbes and Jeffrey H. Mahan (eds), *Religion and Popular Culture in America*, University of California Press, 2000, pp. 201–18.

Robert Putnam, *Bowling Alone*, Simon & Schuster, 2000.

Philip Richter and Leslie J. Francis, *Gone but not Forgotten: Church Leaving and Returning*, Darton, Longman & Todd, 1998.

George Ritzer, *Enchanting a Disenchanted World*, Pine Forge, 1999.

Kenneth Roberts, *Youth and Employment in Modern Britain*, Oxford University Press, 1995.

Roland Robertson, *Globalization*, Sage, 1992.

Martin Robinson, *The Faith of the Unbeliever*, Monarch, 1994.

Milton Rokeach, *The Open and Closed Mind*, Basic Books, 1960.

Richard Rorty, *Contingency Irony and Solidarity*, Cambridge University Press, 1989.

Eleanor Rosch, 'Principles of Categorisation', in Eleanor Rosch and Barbara Lloyd (eds), *Cognition and Categorisation*, Lawrence Erlbaum Associates, 1978, pp. 27–48.

Stuart Rose, 'Is the term "spirituality" a word that everybody uses, but nobody knows what anyone means by it?' *Journal of Contemporary Religion* 16.2, 2001, pp. 193–207.

David Runcorn, *Choice, Desire and the Will of God*, SPCK, 2003.

Tex Sample, *The Spectacle of Worship in a Wired World*, Abingdon, 1998.

Nicholas Saunders, Anja Saunders and Michelle Pauli, *In Search of the Ultimate High: Spiritual Experience through Psychoactives*, Rider, 2000.

Sara Savage, 'Psychological perspectives on the present situation for clergy and congregations', in Steven Croft (ed.), *The Future of the Parish System*, Church House Publishing, 2006.

— 'Sculpting the Self', in Bob Mayo with Sara Savage and Sylvie Collins, *Ambiguous Evangelism*, SPCK, 2004, pp. 172–43.

— 'A psychology of fundamentalism: the search for inner failings', in Martyn Percy (ed.), *Fundamentalism, Church and Society*, SPCK, 2002, pp. 25–52.

R. Murray Schafer, *The Tuning of the World*, Knopf, 1977.

Arthur Schopenhauer, *Die Welt als Wille and Vorsrtellung*, Vol. 1, 3rd edition, 1859; Trans. E. F. J. Payne as *The World as Will and Representation*, Dover Publication, 1969, cited in Semir Zeki, 'Neural concept formation and art', *Journal of Consciousness Studies* 9.3, 2002, pp. 53–76.

Christoph Schwöbel, 'God, Creation and the Christian Community', in Colin Gunton (ed.), *The Doctrine of Creation*, T&T Clark, 1997.

Philip Sheldrake, *Spirituality and Theology: Christian Living and the Doctrine of God*, Darton, Longman & Todd, 1998.

Christian Smith with Melinda Lundquist Denton, *Soul Searching: The Religious and Spiritual Lives of American Teenagers*, Oxford University Press, 2005.

Michael E. Sobel, *Lifestyle and Social Structure: Concepts, Definitions, Analyses*, Academic Press, 1981.

Jackie Stacey, *Star Gazing: Hollywood and Female Spectatorship*, Routledge, 1994.

Laurence Steinberg, Nancy Darling and Anne Fletcher, 'Authoritative parenting and adolescent adjustment: An ecological journey', in Glen Elder Jr and Phyllis Moen (eds), *Examining Lives in Context: Perspectives on the Ecology of Human Development*, American Psychological Association, 1995, pp. 423–66.

Graham St John, 'The difference engine – liberation and the rave imaginary', in Graham St John (ed.), *Rave Culture and Religion*, Routledge, 2004, pp. 19–45.

John Storey, *Cultural Studies and the Study of Popular Culture: Theories and Methods*, Edinburgh University Press, 1996.

Kalvei Tamminem, 'Religious experiences in childhood and adolescence: A viewpoint of religious development between the ages of 7 and 20', *The International Journal for the Psychology of Religion* 4.2, 1994, pp. 61–85.

Don Tapscott, *Growing Up Digital*, McGraw-Hill, 1998.

Charles Taylor, *The Ethics of Authenticity*, Harvard University Press, 1991.

Graham Tomlin, *The Provocative Church*, SPCK, 2002.

John Tomlinson, *Globalization and Culture*, Polity, 1999.

Sherry Turkle, *Life on the Screen*, Phoenix, 1997.

Paul Virilio, in John Armitage (ed.), *Virilio Live: Selected Interviews*, Sage, 2001.

Andrew Walker, *Telling the Story*, SPCK, 1996.

Andrew Walls, *The Missionary Movement in Christian History*, T&T Clark, 1996.

Arlene Sánchez Walsh, 'Slipping into darkness: Popular culture and the creation of a Latino evangelical youth culture', in Richard W. Flory and Donald E. Miller (eds), *GenX Religion*, Routledge, 2000, pp. 74–91.

Brian J. Walsh and Richard J. Middleton, *The Transforming Vision*, InterVarsity Press, 1984.

Pete Ward, *Youthwork and the Mission of God*, SPCK, 1997.

— *Growing up Evangelical*, SPCK, 1996.

Fraser Watts, 'Interacting cognitive subsystems and religious meanings', in R. Joseph (ed.), *Neurotheology: Brain, Science, Spirituality, Religious Experience*, California University Press, 2002, pp. 183–8.

Michael Welker, *God the Spirit*, Fortress, 1994.

Samuel Wells, *Improvisation: The Drama of Christian Ethics*, SPCK, 2004.

Paul Weston, 'Evangelicals and Evangelism', in I. Taylor (ed.), *Not Evangelical Enough! The Gospel at the Centre*, Paternoster, 2003, pp. 137–52.

Paul Willis, *Common Culture*, Open University Press, 1990.

N. T. Wright, *Jesus and the Victory of God: Christian Origins and the Question of God*, SPCK, 1996.

— *The New Testament and the People of God: Christian Origins and the Question of God*, SPCK, 1992.

Kerry Young, *The Art of Youth Work*, Russell House, 1999.

Semir Zeki, 'Neural concept formation and art', *Journal of Consciousness Studies* 9.3, 2002, pp. 53–76.

General index

Note: page references in italics indicate tables and diagrams.

Index of biblical references

Additional resources for youth ministry

These inspiring and creative resources will help your youth ministry to grow and flourish!

Youth Emmaus: Growing Young Christians
Stephen Cottrell, Sue Mayfield, Tim Sledge, Tony Washington

Youth Emmaus is designed to help those aged 11 to 16 explore the basics of the Christian faith. Includes meaty leaders' notes, cool handouts for group members, great cartoons and graphics and a free CD-ROM containing handouts, posters and graphics from the book. Ideal for youth groups or as a confirmation course for young people.
ISBN: 0 7151 4988 1   *Price: £19.95*

Youth Emmaus 2: Big Issues and Holy Spaces
Dot Gosling, Sue Mayfield, Tim Sledge, Tony Washington

Youth Emmaus 2 is ideal as a follow-on from *Youth Emmaus* or as stand-alone material to help young people grow in discipleship. It focuses on 'Big Issues' from the Sermon on the Mount such as living generously and forgiveness, and on 'Holy Spaces', interactive sessions to help young people explore fresh ways of worshipping God. Also includes a free CD-ROM.
ISBN: 0 7151 4048 5   *Price: £22.50*

Accompanying Young People
Maxine Green and Chandu Christian

This book explores one of the most vital areas of youth ministry: how Christians accompany young people in their spiritual journey. Using the 'Road to Emmaus' narrative and the Parable of the Prodigal Son, the authors show how we can be alongside young people and help them to develop their own confidence and maturity in their faith.
ISBN: 0 7151 4908 3   *Price: £5.95*

For more information, visit **www.chpublishing.co.uk/youth**

 **CHURCH HOUSE PUBLISHING**   Available from all good Christian bookshops.